A Handful of Rain

Carol Ward Wilson

First published by Dog Ear Publishing
4010 W. 86th Street, Ste H
Indianapolis, IN 46268
www.dogearpublishing.net

ISBN: 978-160844-507-3

This book is printed on acid-free paper.

Printed in the United States of America

I knew what it was,
what it could do,
how it felt.
When I finally knew
how to carry it,
it was gone,
like a handful of rain.

Acknowledgments

Memories can be both imperfect and perfectly real at the same time. I have recalled the scenes, events, and conversations in this book as accurately as the passing of time would allow. For details I had forgotten, I relied on others to help me fill in the gaps. I have changed a few names for the sake of medical privacy, and I have condensed some e-mails.

I would not be putting the finishing touches on this book today without the help of those who believed in me and encouraged me to keep writing, shaping, and reshaping my story. I am grateful to them all.

In particular, I would like to thank the following: my husband Mick, who loved me through it all and who set aside his own projects every time mine seemed more important; my parents, Dan and Phyllis Ward, whose loving guidance prepared me to live this story; my brothers and sisters, Pat, Dennis, Nancy and Natalie, who lived it with me; Danny Vaughn, whose music inspired my title and who showed me that creative perseverance has its rewards; special nurses Josie Moen and Connie Devlin (wherever you are) and Mary Jane Sprague; writing mentors and teachers Sara De Luca, Judy Polumbaum, and Mary Kay Shanley; friend and editorial advisor Claude Y. Paquin.

for Jacquie

Introduction

I was a special child. Not to be confused with a pampered child, which I certainly was not. "Special," the doctor explained when I was ten years old and newly diagnosed with diabetes, "because you'll have big responsibilities, and you'll know how to do things other kids won't—like how to give your very own insulin injections, how to check your sugar level in a test tube, how to choose your own meals from a food exchange list."

"You'll always have nice shiny hair and pretty white teeth," a grinning nurse promised, "because you'll be eating such a healthy diet."

How wonderful. What more could a little girl want?

Through most of my years with diabetes, what I wanted was to be not quite that special. *Let me give this disease just a little corner in my life, and let me blend into the normal world the rest of the time.*

That is pretty much what I did for twenty-seven years. I handled diabetes differently at different times, sometimes recognizing its seriousness and accepting the challenge, sometimes performing a careful balancing act between strict compliance and cautious leniency, and occasionally living for a stretch of time in complete denial. I embraced the disease, struggled with it, and sidestepped it, sometimes all in the same day.

By my early thirties, I finally had achieved a reasonable peace with my condition and had begun to understand I could manage it without letting it control me, could stand up to it without being angry. But by age thirty-five, years of imperfect control had slowly and quietly taken their toll. By then, I had learned the hard way about every possible diabetic complication.

But something in me—intuition, stubbornness, faith—allowed me to believe I would be released one day from diabetes. I never talked to anyone about this feeling. I thought others would find my optimism reckless and unrealistic. I had an ongoing conversation with myself, though. *If I can just keep moving, someday I will move beyond diabetes.*

This is the story of how I made my way through the early years, barely allowing diabetes a space in my life, how I eventually gave it its proper weight, and how it just slipped away one day—like a handful of rain—when I received the gift that brought me here, nineteen years later, to write it all down.

1

I have always been a skilled and shameless eavesdropper. Try as I might to mind my own business, I always give in to my need to be in on everything. It seems what I most want to achieve in my lifetime is to not have missed a thing.

So in the late afternoon on Sunday, January 13, 1991, while drifting in and out of the haze of anesthesia, I heard words I knew were not meant for me. I was thirty-seven years old, recovering in intensive care after transplant surgery at Ohio State University Medical Center. The room was full of busy people—an aide checking my vital signs, a nurse encouraging me to sit up and cough, a doctor and his student entourage discussing my surgery as they pointed to charts and lab reports pinned to the wall.

I was hoping for a glimpse of my husband, my parents, my brothers and sisters, who had all been waiting since dawn. I was vaguely aware they had been coming and going, but all I could focus on were hushed bits of conversation among the staff.

The kidney is working well and the bladder is emptying efficiently.

Blood sugar is normal and stable, with no insulin injections since noon yesterday.

And then from somewhere in that sea of white uniforms, blurred faces, and tangled voices: *It was a ten-year-old girl.*

There it was, like a front page headline. For just a moment, I was sharply aware that a young girl's death and my life had become forever connected, through my new kidney and pancreas.

I didn't know how to handle this stolen secret. I didn't know if anyone else had heard the comment, anyone I could talk to about it, now or on some other day. I assumed there were rules guarding the privacy of organ donors and their recipients, although they had not been spelled out to me at the time. I did not know how this slip of the tongue fit into those rules.

During my ten days recovering in the hospital, demands on my time and energy left few private moments to think about what I had learned. I had thought my donor would probably be a middle-aged person like myself, someone who had signed a donor card and made a conscious decision to donate her organs. I could have been appropriately grateful for a gift like that, without guilt, without knowing more. Knowing now that a parent somewhere had made this choice for a child already gone, at a time of chaos, confusion and despair, I had to put it away for a while. I needed to preserve energy for myself.

More than five years would pass before I would learn anything more about my donor. Meanwhile, I held onto my little scrap of information, tucked away behind the everyday details of my life. An image of this child, looking the way I had drawn her in my mind, would appear from time to time, always when I least expected it. I would see a mother and daughter in the grocery store and wonder, *Is that what ten looks like? Or is she eight, or twelve?* I would end a phone call with my brother or sister and wonder if my donor left brothers and sisters behind.

Occasionally I would see the aftermath of a bad car accident and wonder if that was how she died. Because my transplant had occurred in January, seeing snow and ice on the highway would cause me to imagine that a winter accident might have claimed her life. I remembered that when I was first placed on the transplant waiting list, a doctor told me, *Be especially prepared for a call from us over the holidays. Winter is a very busy time for us in the transplant department—because of icy roads.*

I had thought it a cold and insensitive thing to say—to guess when and how anyone might die—but it was a reality in his professional world, an unpleasant statistic he probably had to plan his schedule around.

So when those morbid thoughts crossed my mind, I had to keep them from consuming me. It was my responsibility after all, having been given a new life at the expense of someone else's, to keep her spirit alive in a positive way, the way her family had surely intended when they chose to donate her organs. I made myself forget about the day she died and to think instead about the years she lived. I needed to imagine, needed to believe, that her childhood might have been at least a little like mine. It comforted me to picture it that way, however unlikely it was.

2

I was born between two brothers, Patrick a year older than me and Dennis a year younger. Pat was born in Sauk City, Wisconsin in February of 1952. When he was almost one, my folks moved to Whitewater, a college town in southern Wisconsin, renting a tiny apartment on Main Street.

I came along on May 4, 1953. The apartment served us well for a while. It was four blocks from downtown, five blocks from Five Points Grocery, and six blocks from the dairy where Dad worked.

When Mom could no longer lug two toddlers and a stroller up and down the narrow apartment stairs, Dad rented a house several blocks away on Janesville Street. The extra space there prompted my parents first to take in a student boarder and then to have another baby, my brother Dennis, born in May, 1954.

When we turned five, four, and three, that house was no longer big enough or close enough to the elementary school, so Mom and Dad bought a house at the corner of Whiton and Charles. Dad had calculated that if he rented the three upstairs bedrooms to college students, the rental income—five dollars per week from each of five students—would almost make the mortgage payment.

We settled into our new house just before Pat started kindergarten and just in time for the arrival of our sister, Nancy, in September, 1957. Natalie was not in the family plan yet when we moved. She was born six years later in July, 1963, just after I turned ten.

Our new house had every kind of hiding place a kid could want, with more than one way in and out of each, in case monsters or mice or brothers decided to give chase.

We kids seldom used the front door. The girls who lived upstairs entered there and climbed a curved stairway to their rooms. We were only supposed to go upstairs with permission, but I came down from there sometimes with my fingernails painted pink or with a new barrette in my hair, colored pencils and paper clips in my pockets.

"Did they ask you to come up?" Mom would ask doubtfully, and I would hold out my hands to show her my proof.

We did claim the big cement front porch as our own territory, vacating only when one of the students pleaded for privacy to entertain a date on the front steps. Because its cement railing was almost as tall as me and had no openings, the porch was a perfect enclosure for playing and hiding. We imagined it a castle or a cave, a bowling alley or a skating rink. We clamped roller skates onto our shoes and glided from one end to the other, back and forth for hours, with only the tops of our heads visible from the street.

The boys liked to vault over the porch rail, getting a running start, leaping in a single motion—*Ho-lee cow!*—onto the rail and down into the side yard. This usually landed them in prickly flowering bushes and in trouble with our mother, but it was worth it to them. They risked it over and over.

I sat sometimes on one of the flat-topped posts next to the porch steps and did what girls were supposed to do. I cut out paper dolls, wove bright yarn in and out of hole-punched plastic cards, or drew with a stylus on a magic slate. I chose that perch because from there I could watch my brothers and a half dozen neighborhood boys play football in the front yard. I would rather have been down on the field with them, but every game eventually progressed from touch to tackle, so I stayed put, only occasionally volunteering my services as cheerleader, referee, or first-aid nurse.

The detached garage behind the house provided us a short basketball court, separated from the house by a patch of lawn just big enough for a baseball diamond—minus the outfield—and a long, narrow garden.

In winter, we crouched behind snow forts and hurled snowballs at each other. Our black labrador, Judy, fetched and returned the ones that missed. On hot summer days, if we found the clothesline free of laundry, we ran barefoot through the sprinkler. A cellar door allowed us to enter the basement all muddy, to shed our clothes in the laundry room and rinse off under a shower head that stuck out of the wall over a drain in the cement floor. We could usually find clean clothes folded on the ironing board and dress before going upstairs.

At the top of the basement stairs, we could count on finding our mother busy in the kitchen, always within reach of a lukewarm half-cup of coffee and with the newspaper lying open on the table. Occasionally she stopped her work at the stove or the sink and sat for a few minutes to read a column or two of news.

The boys and I shared the attic bedroom above the kitchen for a few years, until we got too big to fit three in the rollaway bed. When Nancy graduated from her crib in Mom and Dad's room, she and I moved into the tiny bedroom off the kitchen, a cubicle only big enough for a set of bunk beds. The attic remained a playroom for all of us, the bed being the only sign that the room served double duty. Mom seldom took a notion to visit our playroom. From the kitchen below, she could hear how we were getting along.

Our neighborhood had twice as many boys as girls, so I learned early on that being a dainty little girl was not an option. Lacy dresses were just an itchy nuisance, and the hairstyles Mom created for me were intended to keep my hair out of my eyes and nothing more. She made tight little braids from the wispy hair around my face and pinned them firmly to the sides of my head.

"Ma-ah, you're stretching my head," I whined, fidgeting and fussing until she released me from between her knees, settled for half a hairdo, and sent me off to rejoin the boys.

Growing up in Whitewater was so easy. No need for mothers to have eyes in the backs of their heads; there were plenty of eyes to go around. My kindergarten teacher lived across from us on Whiton Street. If she stood in just the right spot, her front porch gave her a wide-angle view up and down both streets. Our church choir director lived at the end of Charles Street, halfway to Lincoln Elementary School, so we were on our best behavior rounding her corner.

Mel, the owner of Five Points Grocery, lived across from our Charles Street porch. When we walked the two blocks to his store with Mom's grocery list, Mel came from behind the meat counter, wiped his hands on his white apron, and filled her order. We admired the candy, cookie, and banana displays and played in the aisles, propping open the ice cream freezer lid, leaning in to feel the rush of frosty air. Mel added Mom's favorite candy, a Mars Bar, to the bag, dropped in a treat for each of us, then watched from the front step as we took turns pulling our red wagon toward home.

"Tell your Ma to put those peaches in a brown paper bag on a dark shelf. They'll be ripe by tomorrow."

As young as seven or eight, Mom and Dad allowed us to walk downtown, about seven blocks altogether. Drivers were careful on Main Street. Storekeepers knew children by name. We could go as far as our feet would carry us, as long as our feet turned homeward when the pastel underwater lights in the library fountain came on.

I followed Pat through grade school, and Dennis followed me. With only a few exceptions, we all had the same teachers each year. Pat was a hard act to follow. He was a bright student and a favorite among teachers. I prepared myself at the beginning of each year for the question, *Are you Pat Ward's little sister?* I admitted that I was, never certain whether being his sister would benefit me or make my year impossible.

I don't know how Dennis responded to the question about his connection to Pat and me. *My last name isn't really Ward* would not have surprised me. He made his way through school by his own methods, bringing home a decent enough report card to earn him time to do what he liked after school. He liked designing and building things, taking motors apart and putting them back together, usually with a slight improvement. He and a friend drew an elaborate futuristic car one time and sent it off to the Ford Motor Company in Detroit. He watched for the mail every day until he received the company's courteous reply: *It is not in our plans at this time to produce a car such as the one you have designed, but we hope you will pursue your interest in automobiles.*

Every September, Pat told me what my upcoming teacher would be like. About our second grade teacher, he said, "Mrs. Silvernail is really nice, like a grandma. Only problem is, she'll make you write poems all day long, and if you don't do it right, you even have to work on it instead of recess."

I didn't believe for a minute that we had to know in second grade how to write poems. I questioned him further and he admitted, "Oh, you don't have to make up the poems. She writes one on the board. You have to copy it on paper so it looks nice and fits on the lines just like hers."

Penmanship, not poetry. That made more sense.

When I reached fifth grade, Pat told me it would be a great year, completely different and better than any other. "You'll probably have a student teacher," he said as we walked to school that fall. "An art teacher will come to the classroom. You'll get to make clay bowls and she takes them and gets them glazed and baked. Miss Krueger and Miss Eberle take turns teaching, and they take turns being the principal. You never get bored, having so many teachers."

Pat's advance report was accurate enough, but he had no idea what lay ahead for us that year.

The day President John F. Kennedy was assassinated—November 22, 1963—I was the last in my class to hear the news. I had walked home for lunch and returned a few minutes late. As I neared the school's front door, my friend Mark rushed out to meet me. He looked awful. His face was pale, his eyes wide and fighting tears, arms straight at his sides with fists clenched.

"President Kennedy is dead," he blurted as soon as I stopped in front of him. "Someone shot him in Dallas."

Mark was a serious, intense boy, so I knew this was no joke. We walked into our classroom together. My classmates were all in their seats, looking shocked and confused. Some stared straight ahead. Some watched the door as if they expected the arrival of more bad news. A few had their heads down on their desks. The room was so quiet and so still, it looked like a photograph. I took my seat without asking any questions.

This tragedy gave our teachers their lesson plans for the rest of the semester. We sang military funeral hymns in music class and drew pictures of the President in art class, using magazine photographs as models. History lessons were about the chain of command in our government, about the duties of the Secret Service, about justice for those who kill and the injustice of an assassin never standing trial.

At home, the story filled the newspaper, the television screen, and our dinner table conversation. We had no choice but to hear it and see it and to grow up a little that winter.

We did have our usual Santa Claus, gingerbread, candy cane Christmas. We stayed up until midnight on New Year's Eve with our popcorn confetti. But just as we were getting back into our old routine, five weeks into 1964, three months before my eleventh birthday, I sat in Dr. Nelson's office and heard the word *diabetes* for the first time.

3

It was unusual for me to be in the doctor's office with just my mother, and on a school day too. Normally, a sore throat or poison ivy or some other childhood ailment would spread like wildfire among my two brothers, two sisters and me, and finally, when we were all good and miserable, Dr. Nelson made a house call or we all dragged into his office together. But today it was just Mom and me, and I was not sure why I was there.

As we sat in the waiting room, I made up my own story. I decided I was seeing the doctor because, like my friend Jill, whose father owned the jewelry store downtown, I would be going off to summer camp at the end of the school year and I needed a checkup first.

Mom's quiet conversation with the doctor had nothing to do with my imaginary summer plans. While I studied the body parts diagram on the examining room wall, she reported, "Carol has been sick to her stomach for a few days now and can't keep down food or water. I thought it was the same flu the other kids had, but she's been losing so much weight. About ten pounds in just a few weeks. I think it must be something else."

Dr. Nelson took notes as Mom continued. "For a while now, she's been hungry and thirsty all the time. She never seems to get full. I would think she'd be gaining weight, not losing. And she gets up often in the night to go to the bathroom."

"How long has this been going on?" the doctor asked.

"Well, her aunt first noticed it when she visited there just after Christmas, so I guess about a month."

Dr. Nelson listened carefully, scribbled a few more lines, then looked up at me and asked, "Have you felt tired on the playground lately? Or sleepy in class?"

I thought for a few seconds and responded, "Well, I had to stop halfway home from school the other day. I sat down and rested in Stephanie Brown's front yard."

Addressing my mother again, the doctor said, "I'm afraid what we probably have here is diabetes."

After testing my urine and finding sugar present, the doctor was certain about his diagnosis. He called Mercy Hospital in Janesville, only to learn no bed would be available until the next day. Mercy Hospital was forty miles away. There was a closer hospital, but Mercy had a diabetes specialist, so Dr. Nelson decided we would wait until morning. "Her condition isn't critical," he told my mother. "I see no harm in waiting until tomorrow. We'll admit her then. In the meantime, give her as much water as she can drink, and call me at home if you notice any serious changes. I expect she'll be okay at home overnight."

The delay was fine with me. Now I could go home and eat something, try not to throw it up, and maybe by morning I would be back to normal. Then I wouldn't have to go to the hospital at all.

Mom and the doctor talked a few minutes longer. "What causes this?" Mom wanted to know.

"We don't know the cause, and there is no cure."

I heard their conversation move away from the doorway and down the hall.

Her voice rising, Mom said, "Well, something had to cause it. It doesn't just come from nowhere. We should have..."

Dr. Nelson interrupted, "I can tell you what *doesn't* cause it. She didn't get it from eating too much sugar, she didn't catch it from someone else—it's not contagious—and she probably didn't inherit the disease. We don't know much beyond that."

I heard the word "diabetes" several times, but it meant nothing to me. And besides, it couldn't be anything very serious, since we were leaving the office now without even a shot of penicillin.

I had never before seen my mother rattled enough to visit my father at work in the middle of the day, but that was where we headed.

"You're going the wrong way," I said, poking Mom's shoulder from the back seat as she turned east on Main Street toward downtown. "I'm really late for school, you know."

Mom was silent as she drove to the end of Main, where Hawthorn-Mellody was cranking out tubs of cottage cheese and half-pints of milk.

I watched from the car as Mom and Dad stood and talked in the parking lot. Neither was smiling, and I was beginning to feel afraid. Something was terribly wrong. I could see the worry on their faces. I couldn't hear their words, but I knew Mom was crying, and I knew they were talking about me.

I looked around the parking lot and thought about other things, as if I could will my parents to change the subject. I watched as men in white paper hats loaded square wire crates into the back of a truck. I wondered if this trip to the back loading dock would end like most others had, with a small treat tossed my way. I rolled down the window and shouted, "Dad, would you ask Buzzy to *please* throw me a chocolate milk?"

Dad turned to look my way. He looked at Mom, then slowly back at me.

"Didn't make chocolate today."

Dad left work early that day to drive Mom and me home. It was a quiet ride. I didn't protest this time when we passed the turn that would have taken me to school. All day I had wanted to get back to my fifth grade class, but now I wanted to go home.

When we reached our house, I was slow getting out of the car. "I don't feel so good," I admitted when Mom opened the car's back door and helped me step out onto the sidewalk. I was hungry and my throat was so dry I could barely swallow. My legs felt heavy and I wanted to sit down on the side porch steps. Mostly, I wanted my parents to speak, to say all the usual things.

The dog hasn't been out since this morning.
I'll let her out.
The boys left their bikes in the driveway again.
I'll remind them.

But they were silent. Nothing had prepared them for this day. As far as they knew, no other child in our small town had diabetes. And nothing about my childhood had made any of us think the rest of my life would be any less normal than the first ten years.

4

Our house, with seven of us living downstairs and five college students upstairs, was never completely calm, but it did always seem to run smoothly. We stepped over, through, and around our daily disasters with a routine that had its own momentum.

That evening was different, though, when we returned from the doctor's office. It was completely chaotic. Pat, Dennis and Nancy, home from school already, asked endless questions: *Why did Carol have to go to the doctor today? Why is Dad home early? What's for supper? Can the cat eat in here with us tonight?*

Mom gave no answers. She seemed lost in thought as she hurried to get dinner together. She warmed a bottle in a pan on the stove for Natalie, who sat fussing in her infant seat on the table. Pat rattled plastic keys in front of the baby. Her crying grew louder. Dennis leaned his chair back and forth, daring it to fall over backward. Nancy dragged the cat around, draped over her forearm. She poured cereal and milk into and over the edge of his food bowl on the floor.

Dad kept giving me water, which I couldn't swallow. He urged me to stay awake, but I struggled just to stay upright in my chair. The kitchen was noisy and out of focus. Everyone was in everyone's way.

I sat at the table through dinner, but eating was out of the question. I wanted to go into the living room and lie down on the couch, but my brain felt fuzzy. I didn't know how to tell anyone I didn't think my legs would stand up.

After a few hours of watching me wilt, Dad decided that just putting me to bed was not a good idea. He called Dr. Nelson and told him, "We're leaving for the hospital, bed or no bed."

I remember Dad putting me in the back seat of the car, tucking a pillow under my head and covering me with a blanket. By the time we reached the edge of town and turned onto the highway, I was unconscious.

Dr. Nelson had agreed to meet us in Janesville. He passed us on the road just a few miles from home. By the time Dad carried me into the hospital's front lobby, the doctor had given the receptionist enough information to arrange my admission. Dad was allowed to take me directly to the emergency room.

I have no memory of that first night in Mercy Hospital. I know now that I was given frequent small doses of insulin while the emergency room staff monitored my blood sugar. I responded to the insulin as expected, my blood sugar gradually dropping, over the next twelve hours, to a normal level. My diagnosis was confirmed: Juvenile Diabetes, Type One.

The next afternoon, an orderly wheeled me to a private room on the pediatric floor. I was awake, but drowsy, unsure where I was or how I had gotten there. Told to stay in bed and not inclined to do otherwise, I watched the activity in my room as the afternoon passed in slow motion. I remember having blood drawn, eating spoonfuls of nondescript food, struggling with a bedpan, hearing adult voices beyond the door.

My energy improved through the evening, and Dad assured me, "You'll feel even better in the morning."

"We'll be here as early as we can tomorrow," Mom said as they left for the night. "The doctor plans to talk to us then about your diabetes."

About my diabetes. I wondered what all the fuss was about. I had been feeling better since dinner and couldn't imagine not being completely recovered by morning. Recovered from diabetes, whatever that was.

As Mom and Dad had promised, I woke up the next morning wanting to get out of bed and walk around, to see what was out in the hall, to look outside my window. My stomach wanted real food. I waited for someone to tell me what time Mom and Dad would come to take me home. *Is today a school day? Will I be going back tomorrow?*

There was no time for questions. A nurse came in early and went quickly through her morning routine: temperature, blood pressure, an insulin injection, and a request that I leave a urine sample in a cup in the bathroom. For now, I would be allowed to stray only that far from my bed, but it felt good to stand up.

Then a dietitian arrived with a breakfast tray. It included all of my favorites—Cheerios and milk with a sliced banana, a poached egg on toast, and a glass of orange juice. Someone must have asked my mother what I liked for breakfast. The dietitian stayed while I ate. She had a long checklist of foods, and she read each item, asking whether I liked or disliked it. "It will be very important this week that you eat everything we bring you at mealtime. We have to know if there is anything you'd have a hard time eating."

This week, she had said. So I was going to be here for a whole week. I thought it was nice she asked about the food, though. I was getting the idea that what I ate from now on would be important somehow. I noticed too, on the menu where we wrote my lunch choices, that it was Thursday. The next day was a school day, but I wouldn't be going.

Mom and Dad brought a sackful of my things when they visited that morning—pajamas, slippers, my toothbrush, books, pencils, and a stack of lined paper. More signs I would be staying put for a while. I was resigned to it now. Having some of my own belongings made it a little better.

Dr. McNichols, a diabetes specialist, arrived midmorning. He sat in a chair near the foot of my bed. I thought he was handsome and had a nice smile. In a kind and sympathetic voice, he asked me, "Do you know what diabetes is?"

"I guess so," I said. "It's what made me sick."

He smiled. "You have a disease. You will always have it. You're not sick, but you *are* special."

I wanted to believe him, but I had known people who had spent time in the hospital. They didn't go there because they were special. They were sick or injured. Sometimes they died.

"Special," the doctor continued, "because you'll have big responsibilities, and you'll know how to do things other kids won't—like how to give your very own insulin injections, how to check your sugar level in a test tube, how to choose your own meals from a food exchange list."

"You'll always have nice shiny hair and pretty white teeth," a grinning nurse promised, "because you'll be eating such a healthy diet."

Dr. McNichols laid out for my parents and me our plan for the next week. He spoke carefully, looking from Mom to Dad to me to see if we were understanding it all.

"For a few days," he began, "a dietitian will plan your meals based on your blood sugar level. When we know how many calories you require—we'll start with 1800—we'll teach you how to choose your own food from an exchange list."

He went on to explain that I would be testing my urine for sugar before each meal and at bedtime. "Like a little chemistry experiment in a test tube," he said. "It's a test you'll do at home too. You'll write down the results in a booklet, and when you come to my office, I'll study them and I'll know how to adjust your insulin and diet."

He continued, "We'll give you thirty-five units of insulin every morning. We'll adjust that amount based on your test results. Soon you'll learn to give your own injections."

Give my own injections? I thought he had misspoken, but as I looked from face to face around the room, I could see he had not. It seemed they were all waiting for a reaction from me. There was none. It was just not sinking in.

I asked, "How long will I have to take insulin?"

"For the rest of your life," was his solemn reply. "Every day."

Every day for the rest of my life. This was sinking in.

My mind wandered during the rest of the doctor's talk, a speech he directed more toward my parents than me. I heard words like *lifelong* and *incurable*, but to me, lifelong was the duration of a night's homework, and incurable was a notion I didn't want to grasp. So I let his dire predictions pass me by.

The doctor's next bombshell caught my attention. "She won't be able to eat sweets anymore."

I did not like the sound of that at all. I didn't understand the details well enough yet to protest, so I just listened, turning over and over the idea of giving myself shots and giving up candy. I had heard enough for one day. I wanted everyone to stop being so serious, for someone to put my stuff back in the bag and say, "You seem so much better already. Let's all go home now."

But it was clear by the end of our discussion that a busy week lay ahead for me, a week in the hospital learning new skills that might be easy, might be difficult, might be impossible. I loved learning new things in school, but this would be unlike anything my teachers had ever expected of me.

Dad went home to take over for the babysitter. Mom stayed through dinner. I was fairly certain it would be the last time my parents would be able to visit me together. My brothers were eleven and nine, my sisters six and seven months. Mom would come during the day while three were in school and Natalie was in a babysitter's care. Dad would visit after work, but only on the evenings he wasn't expected at our church, where he was part-time custodian.

It was hard to have them go that night. After dinner, Mom seemed reluctant to leave. She tucked in my blankets all around, asked if I needed a drink of water, and arranged my get-well cards around the room. She would slip out quietly after I fell asleep, I thought, but sleep was not coming easily. After a technician drew my last blood sample for the day, Mom finally said goodnight.

I had never been afraid of the dark, but I asked a nurse that night if she could leave the lights on.

Morning was brighter. I was feeling even better than the day before, and my surroundings were familiar now. The early morning blood draw was over before I was awake enough to dread it. A nurse came shortly afterward to give me my insulin injection. That would be the end of needles for a while.

Two nurses, one with a blonde ponytail and one a dark brunette, introduced themselves that morning and announced they would be taking care of me every day for the next week. Josie and Connie were as pretty as the Barbie dolls I had abandoned in my dresser drawer at home. I knew right away I liked them. Every day that week I looked forward to the start of their shift. They entertained me when I was bored between visitors. They patiently taught me everything I needed to know about managing diabetes. And they consoled me on the few occasions when it all seemed too much.

Josie and Connie let me help them whenever they could get away with it, allowing me sometimes to play nurse's aide.

"Time to change those sheets," Josie would announce as she whisked back my covers.

I thought I was seriously lightening her load as I took the sheets from my bed, carried them down the hall and stuffed them into the laundry chute.

A graying and humorless head nurse noticed our routine after a few days and scolded Josie for letting me handle the dirty linens and the germ-laden chute. "You can't let that child change her own bed! Don't let me see that again!"

We didn't let her see that again, but I continued to help my nurses in less visible ways, carrying my meal trays out to the cart in the hall after I finished eating, shaking down the mercury in the thermometer after they took my temperature, and composing pretend reports for my doctor about my progress. Josie and Connie told me these were very important responsibilities. They made it easy for me to believe them. They made it clear, though, that my hospital stay would not be all fun and games. We would be getting down to business the next morning. I had imagined I would learn about the diet, the testing, and the insulin injections one at a time, getting good at one before moving on to the next, but they warned me we would be diving headlong into all three. I agreed cheerfully, feeling confident now, and hopeful. They believed in me, and their optimism was contagious.

5

Early Saturday morning, my first lesson arrived with break-fast. A plump woman wearing half-glasses waddled in with an armload of charts and booklets, paper and pencils. She eased onto a round stool too small for her bottom. As she arranged herself around its edges, she announced she had come to teach me about diet. She told me that from now on I would, with her expert guidance, be planning my own meals. She talked all through my breakfast, describing how each item on my plate belonged to a specific food group.

"That egg is the same as meat, and it counts as one meat exchange. Milk comes from the dairy column; one cup equals one exchange. Cheese is a dairy product too, but it is consid-ered a meat because it is high in protein. And a cup of cereal is the same as a slice of bread."

"Cereal is not the same as bread," I told her with my mouth full of rice krispies and with more sass than I intended. I was immediately sorry I had spoken.

The woman stopped talking and sighed, so disappointed she would have to start all over. She slowed her speech as if I were a very slow learner. "Cereal is not the *same* as bread. It has the same *nutrition* as bread. So we must *count* it as bread."

At home we didn't talk about nutrition and balanced meals. We just ate them. Mom put something brown, some-thing white, and something colorful on our plates, and we ate it all. We didn't call cereal bread and eggs meat. Peanut butter and cheese were not meat either at our house. I wanted to go home where everything made more sense.

The woman regained her patience, then showed me on paper how the lists worked, all laid out in neat columns on a chart. It became easy for me then, when I could read it for myself. I combined the right number of portions from each category to create meals for the next few days. It was like the story problems we were doing in math, trying to get the calories to add up to the correct daily total. I was enjoying this now. It seemed easy on paper anyway.

Whenever Mom was visiting at mealtime, we learned together about meal planning and substitutions. The dietitian would stop in and tell us how we could work in a few treats now and then. Mom liked to bake and seemed glad to hear she could make cookies with artificial sweeteners, and that on special occasions I could have a quarter cup of ice cream or a small piece of plain cake. Six jelly beans or one large marshmallow, each equal to a slice of bread, would allow me some version of an Easter basket or Halloween goody bag. I was beginning to think the diet thing might be tolerable, especially when I saw Mom taking careful notes about creating sugarless treats.

Within a few days, though, the diet puzzle was no longer an intriguing game. I was often hungry and wanted more food on my tray. I wished I could eat something once in a while just for fun, just because it would taste good. But it was forbidden on this rigid plan to eat anything just because I wanted to.

One day I had chosen cherries for the fruit exchange my diet plan included at lunch. They were the sweetest thing I had eaten during my hospital stay so far. They tasted like heaven. There were so few in the bowl, they were gone in a minute, so I asked if I could have more.

I was disappointed when the dietitian told me, "I'm sorry, but you can't. The portion is small because cherries have more sugar than other fruits. All foods have to be counted and measured, even healthy ones like fruits and vegetables. Remember?"

When a white-haired, pink-striped lady wheeled in later that day with a cart full of magazines, note cards, candy and gum, the first thing to catch my eye was chocolate. I bought a sugar-free milk chocolate candy bar with the dollar bill Dad had left in my night stand drawer the day before. I put the candy on the lunch tray that still hovered over my bed.

When the dietitian came to remove my dishes, she noticed the candy and said, "You'll have to ask your doctor's permission before you can eat that."

"But it's *sugar free*," I whined.

She quietly put the candy in the drawer, closing it firmly. Out of sight, but not out of mind.

Mom arrived just after lunch, followed a few minutes later by Dr. McNichols. He had barely reached my bedside when I showed him the candy, still in its glossy pink and white wrapper, and asked if it was okay for me to have it.

Before I could plead my case, he patiently told me, "Even sugar-free candy has calories. No matter what the source, extra calories become excess sugar in the bloodstream."

Something without sugar can become sugar? This was illogical—way beyond fifth grade science—but I took his word for it. I dropped the candy bar back into the drawer, wondering if he would trust me enough not to confiscate it on his way out.

The doctor ended his visit by explaining that while I was in the hospital, I would have to be absolutely precise about eating only what was brought on my tray. "You can do that, can't you?"

The restrictions I would be facing for the rest of my life seemed permanent and inescapable now, and heavy. Tears were threatening to give me away, so I just nodded. I wanted him to believe I would have no trouble giving up candy, and I wished he would leave my room. He had barely disappeared into the hallway when I burst into tears and wailed at my mother, "I...just...want...dessert!"

Mom put her arms around me and assured me it would all get easier, but I could tell she didn't believe it either. I saw the sad, weary look on her face. I was in for a long haul, and we both knew it.

Afterwards, I couldn't believe I had acted like such a baby, crying over a candy bar. But it wasn't just about the candy. It was about everything happening to me all at once. It was about the hazards that lay ahead, hinted at, but not clearly defined. My life plan, whatever part of it was already in place in my ten-year-old dreams, was slipping away. And I knew so little about what was to come, I couldn't even invent a new one. I didn't worry for long. I stopped feeling sorry for myself after the chocolate outburst and decided I was going to have to learn to deal with the diet. I promised myself I would be good at it. I resigned myself to it, hoping that whatever came next would be easier.

What came next was the little chemistry experiment the doctor had told me about. It was a method for detecting sugar in the urine. If blood sugar was normal, the urine contained little or no sugar. If the urine test showed an excess of sugar, that meant blood sugar had been elevated enough to "spill" into the urine. Since each person has a different threshold at which this spilling occurs, the urine test is, at best, a crude and delayed measure of blood sugar. But at the time, and for about twenty more years, it was the only method available for home testing.

Four times every day, I toted my bedpan down the hall, Josie or Connie following close behind to prevent a misstep and a spill. When I entered the small room across from the nurses' station for the first time, I stood at a counter and marveled at all the jars, bottles and test tubes lined up along its back edge.

"This kit is yours," an enthusiastic technician explained, pointing to a gray plastic container labeled *Clinitest*.

Its three upright slots held an eyedropper, a test tube, and a jar of blue-and-white speckled tablets. The young man showed me how to put two drops of urine and four drops of water into the test tube. He unscrewed the top of the jar and placed a tablet in my hand. "Now drop in one of these, and then wait for the fizzing to stop."

The concoction hissed and foamed, rising almost to the top of the tube before it settled again in the bottom. I stared at it, amazed that a little round pill could cause such a commotion.

"Now tilt the tube back and forth until the liquid is all one color," he instructed. "Hold the tube only by the top edge. The bottom will be too hot to touch."

I tipped the tube back and forth a few times, tapping the bottom once with my little finger, thinking it couldn't really be all that hot. It was. I didn't touch it again. The final color was a brilliant medium blue.

"Good," the technician proclaimed. "That's exactly what we're looking for."

The kit contained a chart with colored squares ranging from blue to green, to green-brown, brown, brown-orange, and orange. The squares were marked Negative, Trace, 1+, 2+, 3+, and 4+, indicating increasing amounts of sugar.

"Blue is negative," the technician explained. "That's our goal. No sugar."

I was feeling confident again—thrilled, in fact—that I had learned so easily how to do the test. To even be allowed inside this mini-lab seemed like a special grown-up privilege. And the goal—the blue negative—was easy to achieve in the hospital. I knew exactly how to get it. No sugar in, no sugar out.

Blue would become more elusive when I returned home and back to a less structured schedule, but for now I was enjoying success at diabetes management. I decided I might add *chemist* to the list of things I wanted to be when I grew up. Right after *nurse*, maybe, and before *librarian*.

6

On Sunday morning, I knew Mom and Dad wouldn't be coming to visit until after church, so I passed the time after breakfast by taking a walk down the hall in a new direction. I looked into a room where a boy about two years old was lying very still in an oxygen tent. He looked so fragile and pale, I wondered if he was going to get well. Then I paused in the doorway of a room shared by two girls enjoying icy orange popsicles, probably soothing sore throats after tonsillectomies. They grinned and waved, holding up their melting treats. The little boy had looked like he might never go home. The girls looked well enough to go at any moment. I wondered how serious my own condition was and decided it probably landed somewhere in between.

I walked to the end of the hall, rounded the corner and came to a room where a volunteer was entertaining three toddlers. One sat propped among pillows in a small rocking chair. The other two sat cross-legged on the floor in front of the young woman. She was reading a fairy tale, complete with hand gestures and changing voices. "Grandma, what big *eyes* you have," she whispered, peering at the children over the top of her book.

I walked on, turned around and came back, straining to hear more of the story. I wanted so much to go in, unnoticed, to listen. I thought I was too big, though, and that being read to was for little kids.

I wandered back to my room. When I reached the doorway, Josie and Connie were waiting there with a tray that held a grapefruit in a Styrofoam bowl. Breakfast was over, it was too early for lunch, and grapefruit seemed an unlikely and undesirable snack. Then I noticed their tray also held a rubber-stoppered vial of clear liquid, a syringe, and a box of alcohol swabs. They had warned me this was coming. The grapefruit would be my practice target for insulin injections. I stood there in the doorway, wishing for a moment I could become invisible, but knowing there was no way around this. I climbed onto my bed and waited for Injection Lesson Number One. I looked more closely now at the syringe and took a deep breath. *I can do this. I can do this. I can do this.*

Bored by now with the kid stuff—twisting stick figures together from pastel pipe cleaners, teaching spelling words to the stuffed animals lined up at the foot of my bed, styling and restyling my unruly hair with a miniature comb and mirror— I welcomed having something more interesting to do. I was ready to get started.

I enjoyed injecting that grapefruit with make-believe insulin. Over and over, dozens of times, I wiped its skin clean with alcohol and stuck it with the needle. I eased the saline solution into the grapefruit's flesh, then put pressure on the injection site with another alcohol swab and eased the needle back out. I used each grapefruit until it had swelled to the size of a cantaloupe, and then Josie or Connie would bring me another. With the patience of saints, they allowed me to prolong this routine much longer than it took me to perfect it.

Mom and Dad observed the grapefruit-stabbing all afternoon, intrigued by the unconventional teaching method. We joked about the helpless grapefruit just lying there at my mercy in the bowl.

I could tell my parents were beginning to relax just a little about my having to handle the injections. Smiles were effortless again. There was laughter in the room. The air seemed easier to breathe.

I was relieved that we could finally talk about something other than diabetes. I needed to hear there was still a normal world outside the hospital. *What are my brothers up to? Do they let Nancy walk to school with them now? Who's babysitting Natalie? Has Ellen called to find out where I've been? I missed her birthday. Is the Center Street Pond still too melty for skating?*

"Ask someone to turn your TV on at seven," Mom said as she and Dad left that evening. "The Beatles are going to be on Ed Sullivan."

"Okay," I said absently, puzzled by the suggestion. The Ed Sullivan Show was a regular Sunday night event at our house, but I wouldn't have thought to turn it on in the hospital.

Just before seven, when the night nurse came into my room, I asked, "Could you please find the right channel for Ed Sullivan? My mom said I should watch tonight. What are the Beatles?"

The nurse laughed and turned on the television. "They're singers from England. Everybody's going crazy over them."

I could tell by the excitement in her voice she was crazy over them too. She turned and said, "Hey, I've got a break in a few minutes. I'll come back if you want, and we can watch together."

I was thrilled that she would spend her free time with me, a kid, watching a grown-up event. I didn't realize at first that she was just as thrilled to have a reason to watch the Beatles while on duty. Another nurse stepped in too when she heard the music, volume turned way up now. A third woman with a dust mop lingered long after the floor was clean.

We stared at the screen as girls in the audience stood and screamed hysterically, waving their arms and clutching their hair, then collapsing into their seats between songs. By the end of the second song, I was standing too, caught up in the music and unable to be still.

I went to sleep that night believing I would be going home and having fun again, not because I had seen the Beatles—I never really became a fan—but because I had seen an audience reveling in their teenage years and three young women just as exhilarated at twenty-something. Those years seemed worth looking forward to.

I awoke Monday morning to a smiling Josie bearing a familiar assortment of supplies. "Are you ready to do this for real?"

"I am."

A few minutes later, before I could change my mind, a new syringe and a vial of insulin—the real thing this time— were in my hands. But I was not as fearless as I pretended. A grapefruit feels no pain. What would it really be like the first time that needle entered my own skin? And how serious would it be if I made a mistake, miscalculating the dosage, forgetting to flick the air bubbles from the barrel of the syringe, injecting air and insulin into a blood vessel? I had spoken too quickly. I was not ready.

And then the saints came marching in again to rescue the scared kid. I looked at Josie in amazement when she rolled up her sleeve and rested her upper arm on the tray in front of me. "Want to stick me first?"

I thought she must be kidding. I thought there had never been anyone so brave. *Is she really going to let me do this?* She did.

It was back to the saline solution one more time. I went through all the steps, more carefully than before, and gave her a perfect shot. Perfect, but not painless. I saw her squeeze her eyes shut, waiting for it to be over. I decided then that if she could get through an injection given by an amateur, trembling ten-year-old, I could get through it too, and through all the rest.

I assumed that before I could go home, my doctor would have to believe I could do at home what I had learned in the hospital. The diet, the testing, and the injections would have to seem effortless. So after Josie's brave encouragement, without allowing myself another minute's hesitation, I opened a new syringe, drew thirty-five units of insulin into it, wiped my upper left arm with alcohol, and injected myself. It was over so quickly and with so little pain, I wondered if I had even done it. But the nurses made such a fuss afterwards, hugging me and congratulating me, I knew I had.

I don't know whether I felt like crying because I had been so nervous and was so relieved it was over, or because I knew it would never be over. I would have to do this the next day, and the next, and the next. Would I ever not hate it?

There was no choice about the insulin. Taking it every day meant the difference between living and dying. No one had to spell that out for me. So I managed the injections willingly and efficiently for the next few days. I noticed that every day, my increasing confidence brought about less hovering, less worrying.

Although I had not been promised a going-home day, I knew it was close when it finally seemed there was little left for me to learn. I had decided it was useless to complain about the diet. The urine testing was easy enough, my consistently blue results earning me praise for following my diet, as if cheating had been an option. And the insulin injections...well, I only pretended they were no problem.

My Oscar-worthy performance earned me my ticket home. On Thursday, my doctor announced I would be going home the following day—Valentine's Day. I was awake long into the night after hearing the news, excited about going home, but already wondering what that would be like. I wondered if Pat, Dennis and Nancy would go to school as usual on the day I was expected home, and if they did, how I would spend the day. I remembered that Pat would turn twelve on Saturday, that he had predicted I would be home in time for his birthday. I thought about what his party would be like. Probably our usual family celebration. His favorite dark chocolate cake with fluffy light green icing, vanilla ice cream on top. Our birthday cakes were always the same, but we chose the color of our icing—pastel blue, green, pink, or yellow. We imagined the colors had different flavors. Would it bother me if they all ate their cake and I had a marshmallow-topped graham cracker instead? Would Mom even have time to make a cake? A little part of me wanted her not to get around to it, but I knew that wasn't fair, and I knew she would find the time.

I didn't dwell too long on the party details. I began instead to imagine returning to a house that was exactly as I had left it. Dolls still dressed as I had dressed them, ice skates still hanging on the peg by the basement door, my music book propped on the piano, still open to the page of my last lesson. That picture finally helped me fall asleep.

"Try to give Carol as normal a life as possible," were Dr. McNichols' parting words Friday morning as he handed Dad my discharge instructions. "Encourage her to do everything other kids do. Don't baby her, but don't overdiscipline either. Find a happy medium."

My parents nodded in agreement. Happy medium was already their parenting style.

We gathered my belongings, and then it was time to say goodbye to Connie and Josie. I almost hoped they were absent from work that day. They had become like big sisters, like best friends. They had watched over me, brushing away my self-doubt and quieting my moments of panic. We were a tearful threesome as each of them hugged me and wished me well. They both signed my autograph book, Josie printing like a fifth grader, "2nice2B4gotten," and Connie in a more delicate script, "Take good care of yourself - always."

An aide helped me into a wheelchair big enough to hold me and all the gifts, bouquets and souvenirs I had accumulated. We formed a quiet parade, Mom and Dad walking on either side of the aide, Connie and Josie following way behind. Not wanting a repeat farewell, I avoided looking back. A very small "bye" caught in my throat as we rolled onto the elevator and the door closed behind us.

7

When we arrived home from the hospital that Friday morning, I quickly found places to stash the remnants of my hospital stay. I put away everything except my autograph book, which I now thought everyone in the world should sign.

Dad returned to work after retrieving Natalie from the neighbor who had cared for her that morning. I had missed my baby sister terribly, so I fussed over her while the others were at school.

Mom arranged my testing supplies on the bathroom shelf, along with a pen and notebook for recordkeeping. Over the next several months, I would take my test results with me to my appointments with Dr. McNichols in Janesville so he could counsel us about adjusting my diet and insulin.

Mom also worked on getting my injection supplies ready for the next morning, when I would be taking my first injection at home. Needles and syringes were reusable then and had to be sterilized by boiling. Mom got out her smallest pan and lined it with a clean white washcloth. She separated the needle and plunger from the glass barrel and placed the three pieces on the cloth. She added about an inch of water and let it all boil for a few minutes, then drained off the water, covered the pan, and left it on the stove until morning.

Years later, disposable needles became available, and later yet, the entire syringe became a single-use throw-away item. But for a long time, I used each syringe set over and over until the needle became painfully dull and the syringe's barrel became so caked with mineral residue, it would not allow the plunger to move within it. I don't remember how long this wearing-out process took, only that the days I got to start fresh with a brand new needle were like holidays. Then for a few days, the injections took less effort and were less painful.

Except for the little pan on the stove and the testing gear in the bathroom, the house seemed just like before. But when Nancy and the boys got home from school, they made a beeline for the place on the kitchen counter where a five-pound coffee can had always stood, filled with homemade cookies.

"Where's the cook...," Pat started. He looked at me apologetically, and I could tell there had been a conversation in our house about not eating sweets in front of me.

I felt I should be the one apologizing. I didn't want anyone—me included—to go without cookies. More than that, I wanted nothing in our house to change because of what I could not have.

Mom paid careful attention to my diet, keeping most of our usual foods on the menu, but portioning mine differently. Before too long, my brothers and sisters were allowed to go back to having whatever they wanted, but they all did their best not to tempt me. Mom avoided leaving cookies and candy out in plain sight, and popsicles were no longer up for grabs in the freezer. Mom made sugar-free cookies sometimes, flavored with fruits and nuts and artificial sweeteners. I ate them occasionally instead of my bread exchange at dinner or bedtime.

A well-meaning lady at the drug store told Mom about a sugarless drink mix, a red concentrate in a plastic squeeze bottle. It was a bitter concoction that tasted vaguely strawberry, but it looked like the Kool-Aid and Hawaiian Punch the others drank, so I carried mine around too and sipped at it. It eventually seemed like the real thing. Because everyone was trying so hard to make my diet tolerable, I tried not to be jealous of what the other kids could eat.

It was a wonderful relief how quickly my diabetes began to claim only small time slots within our days. It didn't totally change our lives, and my parents didn't keep me under a constant vigil. If they had serious concerns about my ability to deal with my illness, they must have discussed it only behind their closed bedroom door. That was where they always talked about the problems of the day—discipline issues, report cards, finances, vacation plans. We knew such meetings occurred because for every issue raised over dinner, a unified response emerged the next morning at breakfast—permission granted to spend the night at a friend's house, allowances increased for extra chores, a decision made about which relatives to visit over summer.

When managing my diet at home began to feel like a normal routine, our family started going out more, back to our usual places. The places were the same, but the details were different. The first time we went back to Baskin's, our Sunday after-church restaurant, the waitress warmed Natalie's baby food as usual, brought Mom and Dad's coffee, large Cokes for the boys and milk for Nancy. Then Mom ordered a small glass of tomato juice for me.

When Dad asked to see the menu we all knew by heart, I knew I would be having something other than my usual hot roast beef sandwich with potatoes and gravy, a piece of cherry pie, and chocolate milk. I studied the menu, trying to make it fit my food plan, avoiding anything gravy-laden or sugar-coated. When I had settled on a grilled cheese sandwich, Mom gave the waitress a few quiet instructions.

"Only one slice of cheese on the sandwich. Brush the bread with only a teaspoon of butter, please. And could we substitute a vegetable for the fries?"

The menu lacked fresh fruit, but Mom produced a small box of raisins from her purse to fill in the final food group.

Our meal at Baskin's went well, but I was sure we'd be scratching other places off our list because of my diet. Dad had always liked to pile us all in the station wagon and drive us to the root beer stand just beyond the edge of town. He and

Mom usually ordered root beer floats or ice cream cones, and we kids always got a nickel root beer in a child-size mug. I had resigned myself to the likelihood this excursion would not happen any more, so I was surprised on a warm Saturday afternoon when Dad announced we were going.

A few teenagers sat at weathered picnic tables outside the little wooden building, and several people stood in line at the window, but we liked to have our treats delivered to the car. I enjoyed watching the carhop balance her tray on the half-open driver's side window. It defied gravity, suspended there in a way I couldn't comprehend, loaded with frosty, foaming mugs of root beer and cones propped up in a round-slotted cardboard sleeve.

I had a vanilla cone that day. A small amount of ice cream was allowed on my diet, and the ice cream actually seemed like a special indulgence, something different from what the others were having. But when I had finished the ice cream and was down to just the cone, I realized the cone was probably not part of the deal. Maybe it fits in the bread category, I thought, but probably not after the ice cream, and not between meals. I didn't remember seeing it on any list.

Although there had been little need for Dad to pay close attention to my diet—Mom took care of the details—he did notice my dilemma. "I'll bet if you threw your cone out there in the parking lot, the birds would enjoy it the rest of the day."

My parents might have looked the other way if I had eaten the cone. There was, after all, still some ice cream in the bottom beyond my tongue's reach. But I chose to feed the birds.

My parents always found ways to make me feel as if the obvious right choice had been my genuine preference all along. They let small things slide. They knew when to intervene and when not to. Their evenhanded, undramatic approach allowed me to think of diabetes as *just one of those things* my mother always talked about with a sigh. *Just put one foot in front of the other and move on to the good stuff.*

I knew it could be worse. After all, in just my fifth grade class, my friend Candy had to wear uncomfortable metal braces on her teeth and couldn't have chewing gum, Mary had a lazy eye and had to wear a patch over the normal one, and Beverly had to wear a bracelet announcing to the whole world she had epilepsy. I looked at diabetes as one of those things, a problem no bigger and no smaller than theirs.

I worried a little, though, about going back to school that first Monday. The boys in my class had gotten bored with calling Candy "Metal Mouth" and Mary "The Pirate," but what if they came up with a name to tease me with?

I returned to school and found I had worried needlessly about fitting back in. Except for the early morning greetings from my classmates—*I missed you. Are you better now? Here, we collected your valentines for you on Friday*—the day was fairly normal. A boy commented, "You look like the other Carol now."

Carol Rogers and I were both short and had short, brown hair, but she was a dainty little thing, and I had always been chubbier than I liked. Now I had lost so much weight, I had to keep tugging at my skirt to keep it up around my waist. Our student teacher, Mr. Stebbins, teased me about needing suspenders. The whole class giggled, but I didn't mind. It felt good to be back.

After lunch, Miss Krueger asked if I was feeling up to reading aloud. I had been reluctant to ask if anyone had taken my place over the past few weeks, reading in front of the class. My grandmother had given me the book *Caddie Woodlawn* for Christmas, and I had carried it to school every day, sneaking through a paragraph or two whenever I had a spare moment. When Miss Krueger noticed how intrigued I was by this book, she read the jacket. It described the book as a true story about a young girl growing up among the Indians on the Wisconsin frontier. The teacher decided the story would be a good addition to our Wisconsin history lesson, so she asked me to begin reading aloud to the class, one chapter each day, right after lunch. I had worried someone would read to the end of the story without me, but I found the book in my desk where I had left it, bookmark still in place.

The shyest boy in our class walked next to me as we left school at the end of the day. Without looking up from the sidewalk, Keith said, "I didn't know if you were coming back. I like how you read without mistakes." He boarded his bus, and I walked toward home, thinking I might like this boy just a little.

Keith could not have known what his awkward compliment did for me that day. It reminded me that just one thing, not everything, had changed about me. What I had been good at before, I would be good at again. Even if I would live with diabetes forever, as predicted, other predictions had been made for me too, every year of my growing up. The successes I was meant to have would just have to find their way around the diabetes.

8

For the next nine months—the time we remained living in Whitewater—getting back to normal was our family goal. There were brief disappointments—holidays that should have included candy, birthday cakes without icing—but I went into spring still convinced my diabetes was a minor inconvenience, a slightly bent spoke on a wheel still turning. There were a few times, though, when I wondered if we would ever be able to set my diabetes aside, even briefly, and be free of it.

The day I experienced my first episode of hypo-glycemia—low blood sugar—I was taken completely by surprise. A doctor and a nurse and a colorful pamphlet had all described for me the symptoms I should look for, and still I didn't recognize the problem or remember the remedy when it happened.

A few weeks before Easter, I walked to our church one day after school for an extra choir practice. I didn't think about going home first for my usual afternoon snack. It was out of the way, and I wasn't hungry. After practice, I stayed until five when Dad arrived to set up a meeting room for an evening event. After I fetched the vacuum cleaner for him from the broom closet, he sent me on my way.

"You should get going now. Tell Mother I'll be home at six."

When I had walked just a few blocks toward home, I started to feel very warm. It was a chilly day, but I was perspiring. My face felt hot when I touched my cheek with my hand. After another block, I felt dizzy and shaky. My hands trembled as I unbuttoned my sweater and removed it. I knew my sweater had fallen to the sidewalk, but I didn't go back for it. I wanted to, but I couldn't make the decision to turn around.

When I reached Whiton Street, just two blocks from home, I didn't recognize the corner where I stood. I needed to sit down, and I needed to get home. My brain wasn't telling me how to do either one. I made it home somehow, but I didn't remember crossing the street, turning left and walking the last two blocks.

When I got to the side porch, Mom had been watching for me because I was late. She saw me on the sidewalk, where I had become so hot and sweaty, I had unfastened my skirt and let it fall. I stood there, dripping wet in my blouse and slip, socks and shoes, wanting to be inside the house and not knowing how to get there.

Mom realized what was happening and led me up the steps and into the kitchen. She quickly stirred a teaspoon of sugar into a glass of orange juice and held the glass while I drank. I sat in a kitchen chair until the fuzziness cleared. It took all evening for me to start feeling better. I was tired and weak, and my head ached.

I was so hungry when I sat down to dinner with my family, I felt I could have eaten my plateful times ten. Dr. McNichols explained this to me when I saw him a few weeks later.

"It takes very little sugar to correct the low blood sugar, but then it takes a while for your body to catch on that it's not starving to death. That's what this reaction feels like to your muscles and organs. Allow the sugar to do its job, and If you can, resist the urge to keep eating."

Normally, my low blood sugar reaction would have been mild and easy to reverse, but because I hadn't recognized my symptoms early and hadn't had immediate access to sugar, my condition had become serious in a hurry. Before I could get help, every cell in my body, including the brain cells that should have been telling me what to do, were in desperate need of fuel.

After that, I always carried a miniature candy bar or a few pieces of hard candy when I was away from home. And I sometimes overate a little at lunch when I knew it might be a long afternoon without food. I had been embarrassed when I learned I had shed my clothes outdoors. I didn't want that kind of thing to happen again when I was with my friends, or worse yet, among strangers who wouldn't know what was wrong with me or how to fix it.

I found and studied the booklet I had been given in the hospital about hypoglycemia. It described the problem as an "insulin reaction" or "insulin shock." Besides not eating enough food at the right times, a slight mismeasurement of insulin—taking too much—could also cause blood sugar to drop. Extra activity without extra food causes it too. And anxiety and stress aggravate the condition because they accelerate heart rate, causing the body to burn more sugar, depleting the supply. It seemed very complicated to me. Complicated and discouraging. Probably I had better just plant myself in the house somewhere so it just couldn't happen.

Mom assured me, "You just have to be careful about your diet. Don't skip meals. Carry something sweet with you. Watch for the signs." She smiled and added, "And don't get so busy you forget to come home."

I didn't have another insulin reaction that entire spring or summer. I quit worrying about them and just tried to follow all the rules.

The most important rule was to take my insulin every day. It was common in the sixties for patients to take just a single daily dose of long-acting insulin in the morning before breakfast and then to manage diet around the insulin's peaks and valleys. We couldn't test our own blood sugar. For advice about insulin adjustments, we relied on a doctor's review of urine test results and a monthly blood sugar check in his office. For the most part, the dosage stayed the same as long as these monthly reviews showed reasonable control. Taking the insulin every day, on time and in the right amount, was not up for debate.

Late that spring there was a day—the only one in all of my years with diabetes—when I could not bring myself to take my own insulin. I sat as usual on a chair in the middle of the kitchen while my brothers and my sister sat at the table waiting for breakfast. With Natalie perched on one hip, Mom buttered toast and stirred eggs one-handed. Because insulin had to be refrigerated and the syringe-cleaning process performed on the stove, the kitchen was the logical place for my morning insulin routine.

I took the vial of medicine from the refrigerator and drew the proper amount into the syringe, flicking its barrel with my finger to force trapped air bubbles to escape through the needle's tip. Then I sat there for several long minutes, needle poised a few inches above my bare thigh, my hand making the right motion over and over, stopping each time just short of my skin. I couldn't make myself finish the task that had, until that morning, always taken less than a minute. I was holding up breakfast, and we were all going to be late for school, but I sat there with my stage fright, growing more and more anxious, wondering how this standoff would end.

Pat got up from his chair and stood in front of me, determined to get me through this. He made exaggerated stabbing motions with his fist and said urgently, "C'mon, you can do it. Just go for it. Go ahead. Just *do it.*"

He kept repeating the words, and I finally started to cry in frustration. "I.....*can't.*"

I usually welcomed the way he encouraged and looked out for me, but on this particular day, it was not helping.

Mom turned from the stove, handed Natalie to Pat, and asked, "Would you like me to do that for you?" Not waiting for an answer, she wiped her hands on a towel, took the syringe from my hand, and as though she had been doing it all her life, injected my insulin. I was grateful and embarrassed at the same time. I knew afterwards I would never ask her to do that again, that I would never ask anyone. It could not have been any easier for her than for me.

I don't know what caused my sudden helplessness that day. It engulfed me so completely, I couldn't imagine where it had come from. It felt like that time on the high dive a few summers earlier, out at the lake where we took swimming lessons. The lake's small end was roped off into two narrow beaches, a teetering wooden raft anchored between them. A high diving board stood at one end of the raft, offering a challenge to swimmers who could make it out to the middle, climb the ladder and jump.

I hadn't ventured to the raft yet, but Dennis, a better swimmer than I, laid it out for me one day. "The sooner the lifeguard sees you swim out to that raft and jump off that high dive, the sooner he'll quit blowing his whistle at you every time you swim past the rope."

His questionable logic launched me without anyone's permission toward the raft. I climbed the ladder and jumped quickly, without looking down at the water or back at the ladder. I made the trip four or five more times. It was easier each time. Then I decided to take one last leap for good measure, to make sure the lifeguard would notice and scratch me off his keep-an-eye-on list. But this time, I found myself at the end of the board, toes curled over its edge, frozen in place and unable to jump. I had looked down. It amazed me how tiny the other swimmers looked way down in the water.

Maybe my paralysis in the kitchen was like my panic at seeing that distance from platform to deep water. It was the first time I had looked down at my reluctant hand and seen the injections for what they really were—inconvenient, painful, endless. And I had no choice at all.

In spite of my doctor's assurance, "It will become so automatic, you won't even think about it," the insulin injections never did become routine for me. Although I never allowed myself to skip an injection and never postponed one for more than a few minutes, without exception I dreaded it every single time.

Later, in my middle teens, when my injections became a completely private thing, I sat in the bathroom sometimes and procrastinated, all of my insulin gear lined up next to me on the edge of the bathtub. I did the math in my head, calculating how many injections I would have to take in the number of years I might live. I usually guessed I would live to be seventy-five. When I was sixteen, the result was 21,535 injections—a daunting, depressing number. But the math distracted me from the needle and allowed me to finish the task at hand.

I did sometimes believe I wouldn't have to play my numbers game to its end, but adults assured me diabetes was forever. Maybe there would be a vaccine or something someday, but probably not a cure in my lifetime. At not quite eleven, I wasn't spending much time thinking about medical miracles. My diabetes just traveled with me day to day, sometimes in the foreground and sometimes tucked away.

My parents added my extra care to their routine without great fanfare and with little discussion about the distant future. They found a balance we could all live with. In April, they encouraged me to rejoin my Girl Scout troop, and when school ended in June, they didn't hesitate to let me swim at the lake again.

Just before the school year ended, a diabetic woman in our town who thought she should give my mother advice about my care recommended a special summer camp for me near Milwaukee. This camp was open to anyone, she said, but it had trained staff and special provisions for diabetic children.

Day camp at our local park had always worked well enough for us, allowing time for the boys' Little League, our swimming lessons, and trips to visit cousins and grandparents. We could walk to day camp, and it was free.

"But she should meet other children with diabetes," the woman insisted. "Talk to them and find out she's not the only one."

My parents agreed.

The camp had everything the woman and her brochure had promised: rustic cabins that slept ten or twelve, a still, blue lake, hiking trails, and blazing campfires. After a brief tour of the grounds and an introduction to the counselors in charge of my cabin, my parents seemed satisfied and left me to tend to my own unpacking.

Most of the kids at camp were not diabetic, but the facility was well equipped for those of us who were. We bunked with the "regular" kids—two or three diabetics in each cabin—but we had a special restroom in a separate building with storage for our testing supplies and refrigeration for our insulin.

A dietitian appeared just before each meal to supervise our food choices and to show us creative ways to make camp food fit into the exchange diet.

My week at camp did not give me a desire to bond with other diabetics. I wanted to belong to that *other* group. All the special provisions made for us diabetics, as necessary as they were, drew more attention to us than I wanted.

The only other diabetic in my cabin was a girl named Rebecca. She was so different from me, I barely got to know her. She floated around in her pajamas like a ballerina and sang from her top bunk early each morning songs like "Oklahoma!" and "Moon River." She had a pretty, opera-like voice, but I couldn't bring myself to pay her the compliments she seemed always to be looking for.

It was not easy to avoid her in such close quarters, but I tried. On about the third day, Rebecca sat on the edge of my bed and asked me why I was mad at her. I just shrugged.

"Is this your first summer with diabetes?" she asked in a soft, motherly voice.

It seemed pointless to explain that I was irritable not because I had diabetes, but because she was singing me awake at six every morning and I needed more sleep.

Diabetes was the only thing Rebecca and I had in common, and even that was different for her than for me. She wanted to sit and share the sadness and unfairness of it all. I wanted to be out rowing a boat. We were assigned to be racing partners on Water Olympics Day, but she was sure she wouldn't feel up to it. I talked her into it, though, because we were required to go in pairs. I assured her that if she could just sit still in the boat and not tip us over, I could do all the rowing. So she hummed and whistled across the lake and back while I rowed like crazy, and we finished in first place.

Our paths crossed often that week, because the schedule for diabetics put us in the same places several times throughout the day, but we didn't become friends. We parted when camp was over without promising to keep in touch. I had been homesick since the fourth or fifth day and was relieved when the week finally came to an end. I was glad to have made it a whole week without calling Mom and Dad to come for me, but I knew I would not be asking to go again.

When I returned from camp, I began taking piano lessons from a new and more advanced teacher. Mom had taught me the basics at home, starting when I was about six, but now she was teaching Nancy, and I was ready to move on. Mom and Dad agreed to take me to Miss Pritchett once a week. My new teacher assigned me pieces I loved to play: majestic marches, beautiful Chopin waltzes, and lively Hungarian dances. Miss Pritchett insisted with her miniature wooden mallet that my fingers land precisely on the right keys. She had the uncanny ability to see my mistakes before their sound reached her ears. Learning to sight read was a slow, painstaking process for me, but my teacher was patient and relentless. By summer's end, I was becoming an accomplished student, although with a very small repertoire.

9

The new wing of Lincoln Elementary School was so hidden behind the old part of the building, I had barely noticed it taking shape over summer. I couldn't believe it that fall when I learned I would spend my sixth grade year in a brand new classroom. When my classmates and I arrived on the first day Mr. Holk, also a new addition to our school, was wiping a thin film of plaster dust from our desktops. Everything else in the room was sparkly clean. It smelled like damp bricks, newly sawed lumber and fresh paint.

"Don't set anything on the windowsills," Mr. Holk said without looking up. "They just painted the last coat last night."

At first, I thought our new teacher was going to be all business. But his next instruction was, "Sit wherever you like today. Stay in the same order until I know all your names, and then, if you like, we can make a change."

We scrambled to undo the alphabetical order we had automatically assumed. I landed front and center. Finally, I thought, I won't be stuck in the last row next to the outside wall.

"I don't have a rule against chewing gum," he continued, looking directly at a boy chomping away. "Just put it where it belongs when you're finished with it. And I only assign homework on nights when I'll have time to grade it. That will be most nights, but not all."

We all looked at each other and smiled. This was going to be a good year.

In the middle of September, Dad announced he had accepted a new job selling dairy and bakery equipment and supplies. "We'll be moving to Columbus."

I immediately looked for our Wisconsin map so I could see where we were headed. We lived so close to the Illinois border, I just knew our move would take us north, closer to one or both sets of grandparents—the Wards in northwestern Wisconsin and the Ainsworths in the east near Green Bay. The shorter drive would make it easy to visit more often.

When it took Dad three days to return from a house hunting trip, I knew something was wrong with my calculations. I had located a Columbus in Wisconsin, somewhere near Madison, but we would not be living there.

"You'll like Ohio," Dad assured us. "Plenty of kids in the neighborhood I'm looking at, and a swimming pool right there in the subdivision."

It seemed rather exciting, and it didn't occur to any of us to protest, not even Mom. How would we choose what to complain about when every single thing was going to be different? A different school. Different friends. A pool instead of a lake. And what in the world is a subdivision?

On my last day of school at Lincoln, the day before Thanksgiving and the day we moved to Ohio, my class gave me a surprise going-away party. Several parents sent treats for their children to share. My teacher knew I was diabetic, but the parents knew only that I was moving. Caramel apples, candy necklaces, and grape Kool-Aid appeared, and chocolate cupcakes with thick icing and sprinkles. The proud students who brought them placed one of each on our desks.

I slowly removed the paper from my cupcake, glancing at my teacher as I nibbled around the edges. As he walked between the rows handing out napkins and straws, he stopped at the side of my desk. In a voice no one else could hear, he said, "Blood sugar will go a little crazy today, huh?"

Mr. Holk was not responsible for monitoring my diet—he had not been asked to. He smiled kindly and moved on to the next desk.

I got a glimpse that day, and I would learn over and over, what it was going to be like for me in a world mostly unaware of my diabetes. The world would go on, and it would always be full of food. Some adults would hover quietly and sympathetically, like Mr. Holk had. Others would think they should stand guard every minute of every day, a position both my parents and I would try to avoid. When it came right down to it, it would be completely my responsibility to set my own limits, predicting dozens of years in advance the adult consequences of childhood indulgence. At age eleven, I had no idea what a long, slow lesson that would be.

I finished the cupcake. I drank the Kool-Aid. I ate the caramel apple. I opened gifts and cards from my friends, tucking into my pocket the steely marble a boy gave me to remember him by.

I wondered for the rest of the day when I would start to feel sick. It didn't happen. If my binge had sent me running to the bathroom to vomit, that certainly would have been a deterrent. I would have understood the cause and effect, if the effect had come in twenty minutes, not twenty years.

My best friend Ellen walked home with me from school that last day, and although Dad had warned me to come straight home, we had dawdled as usual. My whole family was waiting in the car at the curb when we arrived. The car was overstuffed with kids, pillows, blankets and suitcases. Mom sat in the front passenger seat with Natalie on her lap. Dad was already behind the wheel with engine running. There was still room in the car for me, but not for another thing.

I looked at the house and thought maybe we should be taking a look around inside for things left behind. How could the movers have packed it all up in one day? I watched Ellen round the corner toward home and tried not to think about whether I would ever see her again. We had acted like it was our usual parting at the end of an ordinary school day. I'm not sure we even said goodbye.

I got into the car, holding my bag of party prizes, still wearing the candy necklace. I had worn it home to show, I suppose, that I had resisted eating it. My small victory.

I didn't tell about the rest. It was the first time I had ever avoided telling my parents about a slip in my diet. The splurge seemed to have done no harm, and I was unsure whether confession would bring on a lecture or more sympathy. I wanted neither. I wanted to go inside the house. Feeling suddenly uneasy about leaving Whitewater, I said nothing.

A few hours down the road, Nancy—a second grader then—could not understand why she couldn't have the necklace if I didn't want it. I knew I would never eat it right there in front of everyone, so I finally gave it to her.

This would become a pattern for me—making sure everyone noticed when I did well with diabetes management, and making sure no one knew when I failed.

10

My family and I left Whitewater prepared to stretch a ten hour trip to three days. We took turns complaining that it shouldn't take a moving van all that extra time to cross just three states. We broke up the trip by spending one night with relatives on the way and a second night in an upscale Columbus hotel while waiting for our furniture to catch up with us.

I had never stayed in a real hotel before. With its marble-floored lobby, plush carpeted hallways, and hand towels folded swanlike on the bathroom counters, the hotel seemed like a mansion from another century. It seemed a million miles from home.

We thought the drive had been as long and boring as it could get, but the hotel provided even less to do. And we had to be *very* well-mannered, our father said. So by Saturday afternoon when we got word our furniture had arrived, the idea of a new house in a new neighborhood—and sleeping in our own beds again—was sounding better and better. We were eager to get a look at the swimming pool Dad had described, though it would be gated and full of leaves in November.

Despite all our chatter about what we would do first when we reached Darbyshire Drive, I let my thoughts wander back to Whitewater. I thought about our empty house and about the willful cat who couldn't be found when it came time to leave.

"One of the neighbors will take him in," Mom had said without much conviction.

I even thought about the old purple Pontiac Dad had left behind for one of his employees. The car hadn't been driven in months. Its only key had been lost. It was worthless, but there it was, a heap of purple metal making me homesick in this strange new place.

Dad had described Columbus as a city filled with new opportunities for us all. I was starting to believe him again when we finally packed up our overnight bags and left the hotel for our new neighborhood. With promises we would visit Whitewater soon, and with upbeat predictions that we would love Columbus, Dad drove proudly into the new housing development we would now call home.

When I first saw Ridgewood, so completely different from Whitewater, I felt as if we had been dropped onto a new planet. I saw no grocery store, no library, no church. Streets were long and curved, sidewalks nonexistent. I noticed there was no curb where sloping front lawns met pavement. I guessed we wouldn't be floating any cucumber boats down the edges of these streets.

What I saw were several dozen new houses, some already occupied and some not quite finished, on a thumb-shaped piece of land. Not in the city and not in the country, Ridgewood was separated from Columbus by a river and from the town of Hilliard by a few miles of country road. The houses were of about six different designs, their pastel and neutral colors distinguishing one from another. Trees and shrubs were young and bare, neatly arranged by unimaginative landscapers. I didn't know yet if I would like our house, but I was not having warm, fuzzy feelings about this neighborhood. I wondered if anything about our small town life would make sense in the suburbs. I doubted it.

When Dad pulled the car into the driveway of our green stucco split-level, we kids bailed out before he had turned off the engine. We scattered to examine the house. Pat found the rec room and stepped off space for a Ping-Pong table. Dennis claimed a corner in the garage for his future dog's pen. Nancy found a sunny windowsill for a tiny potted geranium that had somehow survived the trip. Natalie toddled behind us, hesitant at first about all the stairs, but becoming fearless in a hurry.

My mission was to find my room. My brothers would share one bedroom on the top level, and my sisters another. I had been promised a room to myself. It was tucked behind the family room downstairs and had its own bathroom across the hall. I knew I was the logical choice for this private space because I was the oldest girl. Still, I felt privileged to have it. The room, with its yellow daisy wallpaper, was perfect for a nearly-twelve-year-old in a hurry to become a teenager.

Although we all adjusted easily to the new floor plan, Dad's new work schedule required a major overhaul of our old routine. His three-state sales territory kept him away from home overnight, traveling by car and staying in motels, three or four nights every week. It seemed odd that first Monday morning in Ohio when he kissed Mom goodbye after breakfast and said, "I'll call on Wednesday and I'll be home Friday night."

I hadn't expected that my siblings and I would go to separate schools. Our little neighborhood had only an elementary school, so Pat boarded a bus in front of our house that morning and rode to Hilliard Junior High. I was surprised how easily he did that—just stepped onto a bus for the first time in his life and went off to a school he had never seen, miles from home, where he knew no one. I was glad it wasn't me.

When Mom took the rest of us to enroll at Ridgewood Elementary, three blocks from our house, we learned that I too would have to travel to Hilliard by bus. So many baby boomers were finishing elementary school in the mid-sixties, suburban classrooms were overflowing with preteens. The school wouldn't hold even one more sixth-grader.

I walked to Ridgewood Elementary with Nancy and Dennis each morning, saw them off to their classrooms, and then waited near the front door with my new friend Laura, who had also enrolled late. After gathering Hilliard's rural students, the bus stopped for us, the only Ridgewood sixth-graders bound for Hilliard.

Going to a school where no one knew anything about me, where my classmates didn't live in my neighborhood, and where my teachers had no advance knowledge of me through my siblings, it was easy for me to avoid telling people about my diabetes. I knew the subject would eventually come up, but at first I didn't even know who I would tell.

After taking my morning insulin at home, the only thing I could do about my diabetes management during the school day was to eat properly at lunchtime. Not wanting to draw attention to myself in a place where I was already the new kid, I didn't ask for special concessions in the cafeteria line. I avoided dessert, but otherwise politely ate whatever was dished onto my tray. This haphazard lack of meal planning, confined to just one meal per day, didn't seem to be doing me any harm. Mom still carefully planned my meals at home, but when I left for school each day, she could only trust that I would do my best with what was offered.

With Dad's new work schedule, Mom now had the responsibilities of a single parent during the week. Her time suddenly spread thin, she and I fell into a more relaxed approach to my diabetes management. I thought it childish and unnecessary to have her sit with me at the kitchen table for my after-school snack, counting out oyster crackers and measuring juice. I knew the guidelines. I could count and measure. I could help myself to a snack without anyone else in the room.

My quiet insistence that "I can do it myself" brought about a new leniency for which I was grateful. But over time, it also brought about a thoughtless kind of eating on the run—an unplanned handful of raisins on my way out the door, a spoonful of peanut butter from a jar left open on the counter, a fig newton from the bottom drawer, anything that didn't require sitting down at the table. The snacks I ate were not way beyond the limits, but the little bites accumulated, unaccounted for in my daily calorie allowance.

I thought I was handling my diabetes well enough to do it with less supervision. We were all spread out now in a bigger house, so it no longer made sense to me that my entire life unfold in the kitchen. I was using disposable needles now, eliminating the need for boiling syringes, so I began taking my insulin downstairs in the undisturbed privacy of my own bathroom. I heeded Mom's warning that I should let her know *before* I ran out of insulin, not after, and I still stored my insulin in the refrigerator upstairs, but otherwise, my insulin routine was out of the spotlight. There wasn't much to it then, before diabetics could test their own blood sugar and adjust insulin dosage at home. My insulin routine was exactly the same every day.

I began to do my urine testing too without an audience, arranging my little lab neatly on a ledge in my bathroom. I usually tested at least once a day, but rarely three times, as recommended by my doctor. I tested when I was home, if I had time, if it was convenient. I didn't readily announce my results.

When Mom asked, "How has your testing been going lately?" it was easy to say "Fine," and leave it at that. Sometimes this was an honest response. Fine. Negative or a trace. No sugar or very little in the urine. But as time went on and my test results became less consistent, "Fine," with a shrug of my shoulders and an evasive tone, became an automatic response, a word that came to mean many things. Often it meant *Fine, the last time I checked* or *Fine, considering what I ate yesterday.*

At twelve years old, I didn't understand I wasn't getting away with anything. I always felt well, so I didn't know there was a problem. I had heard about other diabetics who were sick all the time, often spending days in the hospital trying to get back on track. I couldn't imagine this happening to me. I thought it must be different for different patients, that I was one of those who could get by with a more relaxed regimen. I assumed the amount of attention I paid to my diabetes was enough. I wanted it to be enough.

The problem was, peaks and valleys in my blood sugar were causing damage even then, silently and invisibly, in ways I couldn't imagine.

"That's what diabetes does," my new doctor told me. "It's a silent killer."

He wanted to help me understand that not seeing the damage doesn't mean it's not happening, and that diabetes gradually affects every part of the body.

"It's a creepy crawler," he said with a smile and a shrug, as if that made it all perfectly clear.

Dr. Melaragno was an Italian father of nine who treated patients as if they were extended family. His office was in Hilliard, and he came highly recommended by several of our Ridgewood neighbors. At my first appointment, in February of 1965, in spite of an overcrowded waiting room, Dr. Melaragno spent more than a half hour with me, first in an examining room with my mother, and then in his office with me alone. He had on his desk a letter from Dr. McNichols in Wisconsin, a glowing report about the time I had spent in his care.

Dr. Melaragno glanced through the letter and then read aloud to me. "This child has done extremely well and has accepted her disease with its limitations, without the usual psychological problems which so often occur. Her parents are handling the situation with great intelligence."

So my new doctor expected he would be treating a patient who would continue to do well. For the next fifteen years, I enjoyed a relationship with Dr. Melaragno in which he trusted me to follow his instructions. He believed my answers to his questions about my testing and my diet. He made allowances for my mistakes. Even when my own reports seemed at odds with what he observed in his office, he gave me a pat on the back and said, "Keep up the good work. Let's be a little more careful about snacks. I know it isn't easy."

I appreciated Dr. Melaragno for not overreacting. Although I might have benefited medically from a stricter approach, at the time I needed him to understand and care that I was beginning to struggle.

11

When all of the Ridgewood sixth-graders began taking the bus to Hilliard for seventh grade, I was reunited at Hilliard Junior High with my neighborhood friends, and they became acquainted with the Hilliard kids. Then it was often a treat for some of us to skip the bus ride home and stay in town for a few hours after school. We walked first to the library, where we did enough homework to justify our staying after school. Then we walked to a nearby drug store and sat at the lunch counter in the back.

The waitress never seemed pleased to see us at her counter, swiveling back and forth on the stools, counting out our quarters and hoping not to come up short, knowing nothing about tipping. But she served up hot fudge sundaes and suicide phosphates with a strained smile, urging us to "Finish up now and be on your way."

I usually ordered French fries and a Tab, pretending I didn't care much for chocolate or five flavors of fountain syrup. I had to order something. I couldn't just sit there taking up space. French fries were discouraged on my diet, their portion and calorie content hard to judge, but I considered them the least of soda fountain evils. It didn't matter that I wasn't eating what the others were. What mattered was that I was included in that gathering of popular girls.

I was a teenager now, and being inconspicuous about my diabetes seemed more important than ever. I told myself that keeping it low key was just easier, that it was no one else's problem. But the truth was, I didn't want everyone watching every bite I put into my mouth.

Are you sure you're allowed to have that?

There was not a good response to that, if I was holding a half-eaten cookie in my hand.

I was never sure which of my friends' parents knew about my diabetes. I didn't go to great lengths to hide it, but I didn't broadcast it either. When I spent the night at Laura's house, I tucked my vial of insulin in their refrigerator door and quietly retrieved it in the morning for my injection. Someone surely noticed it there, but no one ever mentioned it.

Parents of friends didn't mention my diet either. I ate moderately at their dinner tables, my only strict rule being that I didn't allow myself dessert. I drew the line there. A real dessert, the kind served on a plate with a fork, seemed too blatant a violation. I was more likely to have a piece of candy from a dish on a coffee table, or to pour a quick handful of Cracker Jacks from someone's open box.

Sometimes I had the feeling that a friend and her parents had reached some kind of agreement before my arrival.

Mom, you don't have to check on Carol. You're not her mother. She knows what to do, and if she has a problem, she'll say so.

I never admitted to anyone I had a problem controlling my appetite. I didn't think anyone could help me with that. As I gained more freedom and joined more school activities, my diet began to take a back seat to everything else. I had realized early on that food was going to be an issue for me, and I always knew when I wasn't doing well with it. I tried to make up for it in other ways. I became the kid parents urged their kids to hang out with, the babysitter and tutor neighbors recommended, the obsessive student preferring homework over television. It was like the time in fourth grade when I had gotten a C in gym class. Devastated at first, because I just didn't get C's, I decided that if all of my other grades were A's, my short legs and bottom-heavy clumsiness could be overlooked.

Now maybe my closet eating would be forgiven too, if I excelled everywhere else.

I often promised myself, *Tomorrow I'll start all over and follow my diet perfectly. I won't eat anything at the wrong time or in the wrong amount. And I won't eat any sweets at all.* I usually gave myself this lecture after an especially out of control day as I lay in bed trying to fall asleep. But like the diets people choose for weight loss, mine would last for a day or two, a week at the most. Then I would gradually slip back into careless eating. My attention wandered, my commitment weakened, and my rule bending began again.

My doctor visits had become quarterly by the time I reached ninth grade. Dr. Melaragno and my parents agreed that a checkup every month was more supervision than I needed. At each appointment, the nurse drew a blood sample and sent it off to the lab. Then she weighed me and took my blood pressure and temperature. Dr. Melaragno gave me a short talk each time, and I listened attentively as if it were new information. His soft-spoken lectures were always the same. *You may be able to avoid blindness, kidney failure, heart disease, and amputation if you strictly control your diabetes. These complications may happen anyway, but they can be delayed with good control.*

I went home after each appointment and vowed again to be perfect with my diet, testing, and insulin. My parents believed, as did I, that managing diabetes would come as easily to me as everything else did. They trusted my judgment and assumed I was keeping it all together. Doctors and nurses, teachers and adult relatives assumed the same thing. Keeping up this image was hard work, but I didn't want to let anyone down. I kept moving, kept achieving, and always said I felt fine, no matter what.

I worked especially hard to get my diet under control during the days leading up to my doctor appointments. I ate more wisely and exercised vigorously in my room at bedtime. I increased my insulin sometimes by a few units to compensate for the extra calories I had been eating. So when Dr.

Melaragno got my blood test results back from the lab and my blood sugar was higher than it should have been, it was not usually dangerously high.

Over time, I gradually ate more and more freely, increasing my insulin from time to time so my blood sugar would stay at a reasonable level, even though I didn't have a way to test what that level was. I was just winging it, hoping for the best.

After several months trying to manage my spiraling appetite and insulin dosage, I found myself at an insulin level almost twice what had been prescribed for me. I was putting on weight in spite of my active schedule, and I wondered how I had let things get so out of hand. I wasn't terribly overweight—five feet tall and about a hundred and twenty pounds—but I could see obesity in my future if I continued this way.

On one especially difficult day, I had to give a talk in English class about the poet Robert Burns. Normally, a few hours of preparation would have been plenty for such an assignment, and normally, speaking in front of the class was easy for me. When my teacher called on me, I stood and arranged my notes. I began by reading part of a poem by Burns, something about the best-laid plans of mice and men. My voice trailed off at the end of the passage, and I realized I couldn't remember anything else I had prepared. Had I prepared at all? I was drawing a blank. The notes in front of me looked like random scribbled thoughts. I muddled through for a few more minutes and then sat down.

After class, my teacher asked if I would stay for a minute. "I'm disappointed that you didn't study at all for this report. Lately you're not doing what you're capable of. That's not like you."

Her words stung. She was absolutely right. If I had rehearsed my speech, it was not there in my memory when I needed it.

I went home from school knowing I had cost myself an A in English. I didn't understand what had happened to me that day, but I had to consider that my blood sugar was extremely high, making me unable to focus in class. If I didn't get a grip on my diabetes soon, it could ruin everything—my own best-laid plans.

That night I ate a light dinner—the beginning of another new commitment—and studied late into the evening. I planned to ask for a second chance to give my Robert Burns report. At bedtime, I tossed and turned, unable to sleep. My mind was racing and my body wouldn't relax. I had felt this way a lot lately, and the sleeplessness was making it hard for me to get up in the morning. Long after midnight, I finally told myself, *You can't keep doing this. You're not impressing anyone by trying to handle everything by yourself.*

It was clear to me what I needed to do. I put on my robe and slippers and went up to the kitchen. I sat at the table for a few minutes and listened. No music. No television. No lights on anywhere. I went up to my parents' bedroom and woke Mom.

"Mom, could you come downstairs for a minute? I need to talk to you."

She got up so quickly, I could tell she was expecting some terrible news. She followed me back down to the kitchen.

"What's wrong?" she asked as we stood by the table.

This was so unusual for us, I didn't know how to go about it. We talked all the time, but we had seldom needed to *have* a talk.

"I've really let my diabetes get out of control," I finally began. "I don't know when it started, but it just gets worse and worse. I'm hungry all the time and I can't stop eating and I've been taking 80 units of insulin, not 45, and I don't know what to do, and...and..."

I was crying now, and so was Mom. She hugged me and said, "What a heavy burden for you. I wish I had known. We'll get some help working this out. I'll call Dr. Melaragno in the morning."

We talked a few more minutes. Mom had questions about what I had been eating and where I was facing the most temptation. Were there too many sweets in the house? Was eating in the school cafeteria a problem? Did parties and sleepovers offer bad choices?

I couldn't blame anyone, and I couldn't identify specific troublesome situations. "It isn't just sweets," I said. "I eat too much of everything, and I don't think about what I'm eating or how much."

"You should get to bed now," Mom said and hugged me again. "Tomorrow is a school day."

I fell asleep without a minute's worry and slept soundly. I awoke wishing for a few more hours in bed, but looking forward to a new day and another shot at Robert Burns.

"Back to the basics," Dr. Davis advised when I saw him a few weeks later. "And don't be such a perfectionist."

Dr. Melaragno had recommended we see Dr. Davis, a diabetes specialist in Columbus. Mom and I sat in his office as he reviewed the letter he had received from Dr. Melaragno. He leafed through pink lab reports and pointed out that my blood sugar had been consistently high, often over 300.

"One hundred to one hundred twenty is ideal," he said, "but for now, I'd be satisfied if you could stay consistently under two hundred. You don't have to obsess about the numbers. Just find a healthy, steady level you can maintain every day."

Like so many others, so many times before, he made it sound so simple. I would try again. I knew I had to.

Dr. Davis leaned back in his chair, suddenly less businesslike, and gave me some practical advice.

"You'll be old enough to drive next year. I'm sure that's important to you. Did you know your family doctor has to approve your getting a license? And then every six months, he has to report to the license bureau that your diabetes is in good control."

I had never heard this before. It surprised and worried me. Dr. Davis was right; I had been looking forward to driving.

Dr. Davis looked at my mother and back at me. "I imagine you'll be wanting to start dating too one of these days, and sometime in the future, you'll want to marry, have children maybe. All of that will be possible if you take better care of your health."

It seemed to me this doctor could read my mind. I hadn't been able to envision my life in the distant future, but I had worried about what it would be like in high school.

We agreed to see Dr. Davis again in six months. I went home with new and compelling reasons to do better.

12

I had thought my study hall distractions—daydreams about dating and marriage and children—were appearing from nowhere, but their timing would have made sense to any adult. It was late spring, I was about to turn fifteen, and I had been noticing a handsome boy who was in most of my classes. Teachers and coaches called him Dashing Dave because of his red hair and extroverted personality, his quickness on the football field, and his habit of wearing bright red or orange socks on game day.

Dave was also the class brain. That was the attraction for me. I was often his opponent in classroom debates, but after the bell, Dave didn't seem to know I existed.

I suggested to my friend Melanie that I wished Dave would ask me to our ninth grade graduation dance. Dave was Melanie's math tutor, so I thought it would be convenient for her to drop a casual hint. It would be easy then for Dave to invite me, knowing in advance he had a *yes*.

"I thought maybe we could go to the dance together," Dave said the next day as he stepped into the cafeteria line behind me.

I was new at this, but I thought I should act surprised. "When is it?"

I bought the fanciest fabric I could afford on babysitter wages and sewed a dress for the dance. The dress made no fashion sense at all, but the material, I thought, was fabulous, all lace and embroidered pink and blue flowers on eggshell white.

Dave and his father picked me up in their Volkswagen van, both politely complimenting my fluffy dress. The three of us made awkward conversation on our way to the school, and finally, Dave and I were alone for our first official date. We danced to "The Sounds of Silence" and "Brown-Eyed Girl." Our assistant principal stacked a dozen 45's on a record player, reversed and repeated them through the evening, and pretended not to be monitoring the couples on the dance floor.

I don't know when or how Dave first learned of my diabetes. I do remember the first time we discussed it. During the summer of 1968, after ninth grade, I rode my bike from home one morning, around the edge of Hilliard, to Dave's house in the country beyond town. We had planned a long bike ride together.

Before leaving for our ride, I stopped in the bathroom, where I noticed a testing kit similar to my own on the edge of the sink. Back outside and alone with Dave, I asked, "Who uses the Clinitest?"

"Oh," he shrugged. "Dad's diabetic too."

This would have been as good a day as any to tell Dave about my diabetes, a conversation I had rehearsed and dreaded. Find a way to bring it up. Describe it as a minor problem. Brush off his concerns, then cross my fingers and hope he wouldn't suddenly remember something else he was supposed to be doing. I was relieved to hear that he was already aware of my disease, already knew the details. I would not have to educate him about diabetes or apologize for its inconveniences.

Dave's father was the first adult diabetic I had ever known. I liked both of Dave's parents right away, but I was especially impressed by his father—his meticulous attention to his diet, his endless energy, and the way he saw every experience as life-expanding.

Before Dave and I were old enough to drive, we often spent weekend afternoons at his house. We went for walks, studied together, and listened to music in the living room. Dave's dad often strolled in, quietly and unannounced, just to visit for a minute. One day he stepped in and replaced our Simon and Garfunkel on the stereo with his Kingston Trio album. "You should expose yourselves to every kind of music," he advised with a smile. On the back porch one day, he waved a newly opened can of coffee under our noses and said, "Sometimes we fail to appreciate all of our senses. Especially the olfactory. Have you ever smelled anything so good?"

For me, this was a new look at diabetes. A man in his forties with a wife, three sons, and a successful career, enjoying every minute of the day. Not just living with diabetes, but thriving. Forty looked less scary now. It looked possible, even likely, if I could just be careful enough.

I found myself lightening up a little about my minor food transgressions and gaining a greater appreciation of the need for balance. When I spent an occasional evening with Dave at Carlo's Pizza, I forgave myself the indulgence, then got back on track the next morning. If I went to the Dairy Queen with him after his football practice and allowed myself a small cone, I went home and took a long walk to burn the extra calories.

I also realized that I couldn't break the rules every time temptation crossed my path. I stopped pretending that if one of something didn't make me sick, then another, and another, would be just as harmless. I began to understand that perfectionism—the all or nothing approach—had done me no favors. Striving for and falling short of perfect control had made me feel like a failure. I finally accepted that consistent moderation was my only hope and something I could achieve.

Dave and I dated for three more years. Spending nearly all of my free time with him left little time for closet eating, those cheating moments I had considered insignificant because they were invisible. Dave didn't police my eating at all—he rarely even commented—but his awareness of how diabetes should be managed made me want to stay on track. In the constant company of someone who knew the real deal, someone who watched his father manage diabetes quite well, I couldn't justify irresponsible behavior.

Forty became my goal. I crafted dreams and measured time around it. *What will I accomplish before I reach it? What will my life be like if I live beyond it?*

I had more immediate goals, though, as I turned sixteen and finished my sophomore year. It was my mission that summer to get a driver's license and find a job.

Getting my license was no problem. Pat had learned to drive while working summers on our grandfather's farm. Long before he got his license, tractors and hay wagons had prepared him to handle a car with confidence. When he became a legal driver, on occasions when Mom assigned him to take me somewhere, Pat would pull over on a straight stretch of country road and let me drive. After sitting through summer school Driver's Ed, I passed the driving test and got my license.

Keeping my license took some doing, though. Extra paperwork was required because of my diabetes. I understood the legal concerns—that a diabetic could experience a sudden low blood sugar reaction while behind the wheel, could become incapacitated and lose control. But because hypoglycemia was so rare for me—my blood sugar usually hovered above normal, not below—I thought the renewal process was a too-frequent inconvenience. Every six months, I took a form to Dr. Melaragno and waited for him to fill it out, certifying that I was under his medical care, in good health, experiencing no vision loss, and maintaining adequate blood sugar control.

This license renewal procedure opened my eyes to a new reality about poor diabetes management. There would be an immediate consequence, though not a medical one yet, if I didn't keep a tight grip on my diet. The consequence would be the loss of my license. In a very short time, driving had already become a privilege and convenience I couldn't imagine being without. Having my license continually on the line was strong incentive to do well.

With the driving privilege came new temptations. On days when I had after-school activities and Mom let me take her car for the day, I was free to stop anywhere I wanted on my way home. Fast food restaurants were just beginning to appear in our area, and it was hard to pass them by. I managed it only some of the time.

There was a convenience store too on my way home, its shelves fully loaded with chips, candy, pastries and gum. I often stopped in to get a cold bottle of Tab from the ice-filled bin next to the cash register. I always looked up and down the aisles, wondering about the odd assortment of items the store sold—cans of sardines next to bottles of cough syrup next to boxes of wooden matches. And then there were the rows and rows of candy bars, something new and different every time I visited. Occasionally, I gave in to a package of Hostess cupcakes, making sure I got rid of all the packaging before getting back into the car to devour my treat. Afterwards, I always told myself it wasn't worth it, that I had, in fact, barely tasted it. I would resist then for a long time, but it was an ongoing struggle. One day at a time.

During a routine doctor visit early in September, I mentioned to Dr. Melaragno that I would soon be looking for a part-time job.

"Feel free to list me as a personal reference if you need one," he volunteered as he escorted my file and me to the front desk.

I had never seen a job application and didn't know about personal references, but I knew his endorsement could only be a good thing. Everyone in the area was familiar with Dr. Melaragno, and the job I had my eye on was at a nearby pharmacy.

I landed the job a few days later. I listed references, but the store manager didn't take time to check them. She had just lost her evening cashier and asked if I could start right away. She would need me to work four evenings after school and every other Saturday.

The job was an easy one. A steady, unhurried stream of customers came and went. I pointed them toward what they needed and rang up their Band-Aids, aspirin and cigarettes. I dusted, boxed, and gift-wrapped their selections from the gift shop at the front of the store. I restocked school supplies and candy.

I learned from conversations I overheard at the pharmacist's counter that I had a curiosity about medicine. I wished my job included some work behind that counter. But the pharmacist was a one-man show. He kept to himself, and he had no interest in providing me any career guidance. When customers were scarce, he would leave by the side door and visit the owner of the restaurant next door. I called him there on the phone if someone needed his services.

"Mr. Neeley, you have a customer."

"I'm on my way."

Our conversations were seldom longer than that.

The store manager was a thin, tired-looking woman. Her graying hair showed signs it had once been red. My responsibilities required little supervision, so after my arrival each evening, Eleanor managed the store from her office—an overstuffed chair in the back hallway, with an old shadeless floor lamp, a water-stained coffee table, and an electric coffee pot. She tallied the daily receipts and counted the cash, drank coffee and smoked cigarettes. She checked on me from time to time and made pleasant enough small talk, but seldom stayed out front for more than a few minutes.

When I had worked for two months at the drug store, just after Thanksgiving of my junior year, I arrived home one evening to find a phone message on the kitchen table. *Call Erlene at Dr. Melaragno's office.* I had probably left something behind at my last office visit, or my driver's license renewal had been returned there, missing some piece of information. When I reached Erlene, the office manager for my doctor and three others, she said, "Carol, I understand you're looking for a job. We've decided we need to add a part-time file clerk. Are you interested in working evenings after school?"

I hadn't expected a job offer and had no idea what was proper at this moment. She was offering me the job on the phone. There would be no application, no interview, and no time for me to evaluate my obligation to the drug store job.

The silence on the line was growing as I raced through my options. I had to say something. "I've been working at another job since September," I said finally. "I'm willing to give it up, but I'll need a few days to let them know." I knew almost nothing about the job I was being offered, but I was sure it was an opportunity I didn't want to miss.

"Finish up at your other job then," Erlene said, "and I'll see you next week about your schedule. Could you stop by after school next Monday?"

When I arrived at work the next afternoon, I immediately had second thoughts about abandoning ship. Eleanor was busy at the front of the store. She had strung miniature lights around the window and was searching for the switch that would make them twinkle. She had moved a set of lighted, mirrored shelves closer to the door and had carefully arranged tiny crystal figurines on them—skating penguins and silver-winged angels. She was humming.

Eleanor seemed glad to see me. "Okay, here's what we need to do," she said, a little out of breath. I could see that Christmas was probably what brought her to life once a year.

I moved all the candles and music boxes to shelves near the aisle and cleared a round table in the front window for a two-foot ceramic pear tree. I assembled the tree and looped through its branches a partridge, five gold rings, and ten other sets of ornaments. The pear tree project took most of the evening.

I was slow to gather my belongings that night. Eleanor waited at the door, key already in the lock, while I put on my coat and gloves. It would not be any easier tomorrow, I decided, to make my announcement. Putting it off another day would mean a second sleepless night for me.

"I've been offered another job," I blurted.

Eleanor took a step back from the door and waited for me to continue.

I hurried on. "It's a job in a doctor's office, filing charts. It's right across the street from school. I can walk there. I'm so sorry, but I really want to take this job."

"It's okay," she said with a resigned smile. "It sounds like a good job for you." She was looking tired again. Tired of training cashiers, I imagined. Tired of working with the silent pharmacist.

I had expected Eleanor to be angry or indifferent about my news. Her kindness surprised me. It made me feel selfish. I briefly considered that I could still change my mind, take it all back. *Never mind. I don't know what I was thinking.*

Instead I offered, "My friend Laura is looking for a job. Can she come and talk to you about taking my place?"

That Saturday I showed Laura everything she needed to know—how to work the cash register and stock shelves, where to find Windex and paper towels, how to summon the pharmacist.

13

I reported for work at Hilliard Medical Arts the following Tuesday after school. Within just a few days, any lingering doubts about quitting the drug store job had disappeared. Having been a frequent patient in this office for five years, I already knew my own doctor very well. I knew the other doctors, nurses, and receptionists too, some on a first name basis.

Judy and Alice explained what my responsibilities would be. The filing system was simple and logical. Each afternoon I refiled the charts used for that day's appointments. Then I made a list of the next day's patients from the appointment book. I pulled those files and arranged them, by doctor and by appointment time, and left them in four stacks for the following morning. Occasionally I tracked down charts that had gone missing—buried in a doctor's to-do basket, left at the nurses' station with a message attached, or waiting in the back office for insurance approval.

On most days, though, I finished the filing in an hour and asked for more work. I was willing to take on more responsibilities, and the receptionists were willing to slide some my way. I learned how to file lab reports, making sure they landed first on a doctor's desk for review. I answered the phone and made appointments or took messages, recorded payments received in the mail, and occasionally called a pharmacy with refill information.

As I glanced through the papers I filed and absorbed the conversations occurring all around me, I knew I was being exposed to information not normally entrusted to sixteen-year-olds. There was an expectation, unspoken but clearly understood, that I would honor the privacy of patients. Many were my classmates, teachers, friends and neighbors. I learned to separate names from diagnoses. I pretended not to know that one of my teachers' insides were backward, heart on the right and appendix on the left, and that a family in our neighborhood was being overly optimistic about their son's bone cancer.

I wasn't tempted to repeat what I read or heard at work. I was drawn, though, to medical information. I read everything I had time for: medical reports, hospital discharge summaries, drug pamphlets, letters from specialists. I jotted down unfamiliar terms and looked them up in the massive medical dictionary on the transcriptionist's shelf. I leafed through the Physicians' Desk Reference for pictures and descriptions of unfamiliar drugs, memorizing what they looked like, their uses and their side effects.

If anyone noticed I was helping myself to a free medical education, no one seemed to mind. Doctors and nurses readily answered my questions, either in passing at the front desk or at day's end in one of their offices.

Ours was a busy office, impossible to keep on schedule, its waiting room sometimes offering standing room only. In the two years I worked there, I saw hundreds of patients come and go, in various stages of illness and recovery, injury and repair, optimism and despair. Among them, I saw for the first time the life-changing complications of diabetes. Our doctors treated few Type One diabetics because pediatrics was not a specialty in our building. Our diabetic patients were mostly older, with Type Two, adult-onset diabetes. I knew the differences between the two, Type One being of sudden onset and requiring immediate treatment with insulin injections, Type Two developing more slowly and taking longer to diagnose, requiring insulin only when diet alone isn't enough. Type One is thought to be viral in nature, Type Two hereditary or caused by obesity and poor diet.

But the complications are the same. I was seeing them up close for the first time. It was unavoidable. Reading about possible complications when I was ten—when they still seemed distant and unlikely—and seeing them now firsthand were two very different things. I could not easily disregard what was right in front of me.

One of our diabetic patients was a teacher I especially liked, a divorcee nearing retirement. He had a son about my age who drove for him because he was losing his vision. He struggled with recurring foot infections, ulcers that took months to heal and made it difficult for him to walk in traditional shoes.

Mr. Shelton was fond of one of our older nurses. He complimented and flirted with Margie, unconcerned about who was listening. In private, he asked her over and over to go out with him. A few times he suggested they should get married.

Margie dismissed his proposals lightly and with kindness. Although I think she liked Mr. Shelton very much, she wouldn't consider a life with him. "Because he just *refuses* to take care of himself," she told us. "I don't want to outlive another husband."

I wanted to defend Mr. Shelton, to explain to Margie that it just isn't that easy. Diabetes was aging Mr. Shelton in a hurry. He still had a son to raise, a son who was already having to care for him. And it looked like late-life romance would elude him. I didn't think he was refusing to take care of himself. I thought he sometimes just didn't see the use.

Feeling sorry for Mr. Shelton allowed my own fears to surface. Maybe I too would have a child one day who needed raising, but who would have to look after me instead. Maybe marriage itself would be out of the question, my Prince Charming deciding after careful deliberation that life would be easier with a healthy wife.

Usually these moments of self-doubt were sudden and brief, disappearing soon after Mr. Shelton left the office. Most of the time I could not imagine ending up in his condition. I still felt disconnected from other diabetics, especially those who were older, those for whom time itself had added to the damage of diabetes.

Only when it was time for my routine appointments with Dr. Melaragno did my own diabetes receive any attention in the office. I felt well every day. Even on days when I hadn't been especially vigilant about food, my energy level was high. The staff were a nurturing and protective bunch, and yet, as aware as they were of my condition and as knowledgeable about diabetes in general, they felt little need to watch my diet or give advice. Except for the occasional edible bribe brought in by pharmaceutical salesmen—a box of chocolates or a tin of imported cookies—there were few temptations lying around the office. Diet soft drinks had become commonplace, so I frequented the waiting room vending machine, thriving on the caffeine in ice-cold bottles of Tab. My diabetes was, for the most part, under good control without much effort.

As my high school graduation neared, I kept thinking how easy life would be if I could stay right there in that office doing my filing job. My days were nice and tidy, my responsibilities all lined up for me like those bright-colored folders along the wall. But I had always been, first and foremost, an avid student, and I couldn't imagine suddenly not being one. College was on the agenda for me. It seemed I had been preparing for it all my life.

Not at all sure I wanted or needed a degree, I shopped casually and halfheartedly for a college. The medical profession seemed a comfortable choice for me. I admired the professionals I worked with and imagined myself among them. The nurses encouraged me to join their ranks, each recommending her own alma mater. One of the doctors in the office told me he was planning to eventually have a lab on the premises so test results would be more immediate. He suggested I get a degree in medical technology and return to manage his lab. His proposal sounded like such a simple plan. I seriously considered it.

During my senior year, I met often with my guidance counselor, not because I was ever in agreement with his suggestions, but because he had all the college catalogs and financial aid materials in one place. One-stop shopping for a girl running out of time. His career goals for me were loftier than my own. When I said *lab tech*, he heard *microbiologist*. My *pediatric nurse* quickly became his *pediatrician*. Using the word *waste* more than once, he implied that the careers I was considering were for average students.

I rebelled one day in my counselor's office, crossing my arms and announcing, "What I might really want to be is a writer." I waited for him to throw his hands in the air and tell me my time was up. Not easily deterred, he patiently gathered from his shelves an array of catalogs from prestigious liberal arts schools—Barnard and Wellesley and Smith. Expensive New England women's colleges I didn't even mention to my parents.

Enrollment deadlines were approaching and I was getting no closer to a decision when my rescue arrived one day in the mail. Texas Christian University in Fort Worth sent me a letter offering me a generous scholarship and admission to their nursing program. I had applied there early on, when a nursing career had seemed a likely choice. They had just received my scores from the National Merit Scholarship test I had taken months earlier and had forgotten about. TCU had a highly acclaimed four-year nursing school, but it was a liberal arts college as well, so I knew I could earn a degree there even if I changed my mind about nursing. TCU's brochures displayed a serenely beautiful campus, the Southwest was territory I had never explored, and this unexpected scholarship was making it possible for me to go.

14

In late August, 1971, I went off to college well-prepared academically, but with some naive notions about leisure time, a social life, and the cost of haircuts and laundry detergent. I had also failed to envision the details of managing my diabetes in completely new surroundings. I had given no thought at all to how different it would be in a place full of strangers. By choice, I had been a loner while tending to it at home. Now I wouldn't have even those few people with whom I had shared the details of my disease, those close friends and family who had kept a distant, protective vigil over my well-being. On foreign terrain, with no one the wiser, I would have to decide who really needed to know. Everyone? No one? Just my roommates? Just the doctor on staff? It was my choice, and I took a good long time making it.

My parents drove me to Fort Worth, a two-day, 950-mile trip, with Nancy and Natalie in tow. Pat and Dennis stayed behind with summer jobs and the Plymouth Barracuda they had just bought together.

We hauled to the third floor of Foster Dormitory all the gear I had imagined I would need that first semester. I pictured myself spending weekends making new clothes on my portable sewing machine, reading the crateful of books I hadn't found time for that summer, and practicing my old recital pieces on a deserted piano somewhere. I didn't know I wouldn't find time for any of that. The sewing machine would take up space in my overstuffed closet, my box of paperbacks would prop open the window on breezy days, and Bach and Beethoven would stay put in my desk drawer.

My family stayed in Fort Worth for a few days while I settled into the dorm and attended freshman orientation. Dad located a nearby bank and opened a checking account for me with a hundred dollars. Mom arranged my clothes in my closet and drawers and hung a shower curtain in the tiny bathroom connecting my room to the one next door. She toured the dorm to find laundry room, refrigerator, telephone and fire escape.

When it was time for my family to go, our farewell was brief. It was barely daylight when my sisters made a quick exit from the dorm lobby to the car, eager to get moving, to revisit that hotel with the indoor-outdoor pool. After quick hugs from my parents, sisters leaning out of the car window to wave goodbye, I stood on the sidewalk outside my dorm's back door, suddenly and completely on my own.

I didn't mind having the rest of the day to myself. My roommate and suitemates must be upperclassmen, I thought, since they hadn't arrived early with the freshman crowd. I busied myself for a while arranging and rearranging my desk, closet and drawers. I had brought way too much stuff, and I was trying to decide if I was taking up more than my share of space. The bathroom would be especially crowded, with its counterless sink, the medicine cabinet barely big enough for a few toothbrushes and a can of Comet, and only two small towel racks.

I was getting hungry by late morning. I decided to find lunch somewhere on campus, something quick so I wouldn't miss the arrival of my roommates. While rounding up my room key and meal ticket, I noticed I had left my insulin on the edge of the tub after using it that morning. It had to be kept cool, and the cooler I had brought it in was now on its way back to Ohio. I went down to the second floor to find the kitchenette Mom had told me about. I found the room unlocked, vacant except for an ancient white stove, an electric can opener, and a short, cactus-green refrigerator. I stashed the vial of insulin behind the rolldown lid of the butter compartment in the refrigerator door.

Back in my room—still no roommates—I took another look around. I went into the bathroom, straightened the shower curtain and applied lip gloss at the mirror.

As an afterthought, I retrieved the used syringe I had discarded in the wastebasket under the sink and put it instead in the one under my desk. I didn't want my roommates to be introduced to my diabetes, with all its distasteful paraphernalia, before they were introduced to me. There would be a better time to tell them, I thought. Two months into the semester, I still hadn't found it.

I immersed myself in dorm life and in my studies. The basic required courses—designed, I decided, to ease freshmen into college life without scaring them off—didn't take up much of my time outside of class. Still, I read and studied late into the night to make sure I didn't fall even a little behind.

I got to know all the girls on my wing, an even mix of black and white freshmen and upperclassmen. Many were nursing majors like myself.

My roommate, Cathy, was a quiet, pretty sophomore who spent little time in our room. She dated a lot and was active in her sorority. She lived in the dorm only until a mid-semester vacancy provided her a room at her sorority house. Most of the time, I liked having the room to myself. I had enjoyed that kind of privacy at home.

My suitemates, Debbie and Kathy, were second-year nursing and speech pathology majors. They fell into an easy routine as soon as they arrived, having shared the same room the year before. They unpacked their belongings in minutes without discussion about what would go where. We got along well, but they had a social life already in place, and I didn't try to become part of it.

It was a first for me, having to create a social life for myself. Always having been included in several groups of girlfriends, not completely tied to any, and always attached to a steady boyfriend, I didn't really know how to go about it.

Dave and I had parted at the end of summer when he followed his scholarship to Yale and I headed south. We didn't make a commitment, except to "write when you can," but we didn't break up either. He thought we had. I thought we hadn't. I wrote to Dave as often as I could, in language that implied our separation was just a temporary inconvenience. I didn't consider dating that first semester.

Surprised and disappointed that I was feeling adrift at a time I thought should be the best time of my life, I began to fill my hours with any activity I could find that didn't cost money. I volunteered at an off-campus telephone counseling service, *The Listening Ear,* a referral hotline sponsored by a local church. I took my classes in the morning, studied in the afternoon, and offered proofreading and typing help to students short on time—the girls on my wing who had a social life.

I still had extra time on my hands. I was also beginning to dread writing home every time I needed money for a textbook or a new pair of jeans. I took a job in the campus infirmary, the overnight shift three nights a week. We seldom had phone calls or drop-ins at night, and rarely an overnight patient, so my responsibilities were few. The elderly nurse and I tried to keep each other awake at the dimly lit front desk. We took turns strolling down the hallway to the kitchen for a cup of coffee or a snack. My studying didn't occupy enough of the night, and the complete silence was eerily depressing.

My work schedule completely altered my sleep, my eating schedule, and my diabetes management. I just kept myself in motion, ate what I could digest on the run, and slept when nothing else was demanding my time. I did my testing and took my insulin very early in the morning, slipping out quietly in the dark to retrieve my insulin from downstairs, hurrying through the routine before roommates could awaken and interrupt my bathroom privacy.

The crazy schedule was oddly energizing—the lack of sleep, the unstructured meals, the running up and down the dorm stairs all day. I assumed this was what college life was all about.

The life should have included a few parties, some time away from campus, and opportunities to make closer friends. I didn't allow myself those distractions. I was driven to succeed, as if I had to keep proving I was worthy of my scholarship. It never occurred to me that success at managing my diabetes might have been a more life-changing accomplishment than making the dean's list.

About two months into the semester, I was sitting at my desk on a rainy Saturday writing a postcard to a friend back home when Debbie knocked lightly on the bathroom door and came through to my room. She sat on the edge of my bed and waited for me to look up. Her expression was a mixture of embarrassment and apprehension. She opened her mouth to speak, but she didn't know how to begin. I thought she might change her mind and leave the room.

"My gosh, Debbie, what is it?" I asked, expecting her to ask an impossible favor or confess an unforgivable sin.

She spoke slowly, studying me carefully. "I found a used syringe in the bathroom. Is it yours?"

I was so unprepared for this, all I could say was, "When?"

What I really wondered was how long my secrecy had allowed her to think I was using IV drugs. It was the early seventies, and although I had seen no sign of illegal drugs in our dorm, I knew that some unlikely students were beginning to experiment. I could see that Debbie suspected I was one of them and that she didn't want to believe it. Only that could explain the look on her face.

I turned my chair toward her. "I'm diabetic. I take insulin."

Our eyes met again. Debbie's were shiny with tears, filled with sympathy and relief. I felt terrible that I hadn't brought it up myself and spared her this awkwardness. But like a child whose mother finds a two-week-old note from the principal stuck deep in a pocket, it wouldn't help now to say *I was going to tell you when the time was right.*

I should have laid it out for Debbie right from the start. She was a dedicated nursing student who could have been—would gladly have been—an understanding ally. But I had never had one of those, beyond my immediate family, so I didn't know how to ask.

Debbie was far enough along in the nursing curriculum to be taking courses in nutrition and metabolic disease. Her mother was a nurse too, so Debbie had grown up understanding the language of medicine. She didn't have questions about the inner workings of the diabetic body. She wanted to know if I was taking care of myself.

Do you know how dangerous it is to have a low blood sugar reaction without anyone knowing what to do for you?

Do you wear a medic alert bracelet or carry a card?

Do you take your insulin every day? And do you test your urine?

There was no scolding in her tone, but I felt it anyway, because I was expecting it.

Then another thought occurred to Debbie, the one I knew was coming.

"I've seen you have a chocolate milkshake for lunch," she said. "Is that really okay?"

Of course it wasn't okay. I was at a loss for words. Responding seemed pointless. I didn't make the excuse that the wait in the main cafeteria was always too long, and that I wasn't crazy about all the barbecue, boiled okra, and cornbread they served there. I didn't explain that in the ten minutes I allowed myself between morning classes and afternoon study time, I just made a quick stop at the snack bar, stood at the back of the shortest line, and ordered whatever was offered at the front of it. I didn't say anything. I was silently thanking Debbie for not reporting her original suspicions to our dorm mother. When she left the room, she seemed content that she had at least cleared the air and invited me to confide in her.

I thought about our conversation for a long time. Trying to sort out exactly why I hadn't felt I could tell even one person about my diabetes, I realized I had always done this. I had always tried to spare others the inconvenience of my disease. I didn't want any part of it to compromise my to-do list, and I didn't want it to interfere with anyone else's. My goal was to live seamless days, making them look effortless and keeping my diabetes from coming up through the cracks.

Mission accomplished, until the fall of my sophomore year. I had wrapped up my exams in May, satisfied with my first year. I had cruised through it feeling quite well in spite of my lack of sleep and nutrition. No sick days and no emergency visits to the infirmary. I had aced all of my classes except gymnastics, for which I had the aptitude of a turtle.

I went home for the summer and worked full time at an ice cream and popsicle factory. Not an ideal job for an easily tempted diabetic, but a job nonetheless. It was good money, and I could start right away. I stood all day feeding large trays of cardboard tubes into a revolving trough, coaxing them under a spout that filled them with orange sherbet. The machine added a stick and a polka-dot peel-off paper lid, and off they went into a box, a larger carton, and finally into a subzero walk-in freezer.

The long hours at the factory—longer by midsummer when ice cream demand outweighed our supply—allowed me again to slight my diabetes management. The food we consumed during the day did it no favors either. Our half-hour lunches were usually oversized sandwiches fetched from the nearby Big Boy Restaurant or the sub place down the street. On days when machines had been breaking down all morning, leaving us scrambling to get back up to speed, lunches were cut short. On those days, our sandwiches were ice cream sandwiches rescued from the melting mess that piled up during repairs.

My blood sugar must have been sky high much of the time. Exactly how high, I didn't know. Taking my morning insulin on time every day was as good as it got that summer. I always felt well, so I assumed that was good enough.

I dated one of the line foremen toward the end of summer, having finally caught on that Dave had moved on to an Ivy League relationship. Barry was four years older than I and had earned a college degree, but he had joined that group of students who continue living after graduation on the fringe of campus life, prolonging their search for true meaning and not in a hurry to shave clean and type a resumé. Barry's lifestyle intrigued me. He flattered me by saying I was out of his league. I mistook the intrigue and flattery for love.

15

In late August, I left Barry behind at the popsicle place and returned to school, promising I'd keep in touch, assuming we would continue dating when I returned home for the holidays.

I settled back into the same room in Foster Dorm. I searched through the course catalog, eager to get beyond basic classes, pleased to have more freedom this year to choose. Debbie and Kathy also returned to the room next door. It was a relief to find most things unchanged.

My new roommate Jenny was a freshman with long, auburn hair and a deep Florida tan. She was from a wealthy Miami family, listed in the Miami social register, she told me first thing. "They want me to settle down at a nice Christian school."

Jenny was not easily settled. She wore glasses with rose-colored lenses and faded jeans with knee-high boots. She was bright and had an animated, quick wit, but her attention was all over the place. I knew within days I'd be studying away from our room.

Jenny came complete with a small refrigerator, a stereo, and a two-burner hot plate. We instantly had our own snack bar. That brought on the inevitable roaches, the giant Texas variety that can sense an open food container and climb three flights to find it.

I liked Jenny, though, and couldn't help lightening up a little when she was around. We shared food and soft drinks without keeping track. Occasionally we traded clothes—her leather jacket for my turquoise London Fog trench coat, which she thought looked mysterious with her pink glasses.

I mentioned my diabetes to Jenny offhandedly one day. "You were up awfully early today," she said.

"I have to take an insulin injection and test my urine every day. I try to get into the bathroom early in the morning before everyone else needs in," I explained, as if the most serious problem I faced was scheduling alone time in the bathroom.

Jenny responded by telling me about her friend who gave herself weekly allergy shots. "I saw her do it once and I almost threw up."

I decided I had better spare Jenny the sight of my needles, test tubes, and collection cups.

Mornings were easier, now that I could store my insulin in the mini-fridge. We could make oatmeal in our room or have a quick sandwich there when there was no time for breakfast or lunch. I kept cold Diet Dr. Pepper on hand in lieu of sugary drinks.

I thought I was doing well that fall. I was getting more sleep, having given up the infirmary job for an early evening shift at the library. I was eating healthier food and fewer sweets, although the fast food places near campus lured me in more often than I cared to admit.

Three days before Halloween, my paternal grandfather, Grandpa Curly, had a heart attack while pheasant hunting. He survived the night, but died the next morning. I dropped everything, flew home to Columbus, and joined my parents and siblings for the drive to Wisconsin. Altogether I was gone only six days, but the trip was the beginning of the end of my college career. My mother's father, Grandpa Henry, had died the year before in September. His death from cancer had been expected, and that trip to Wisconsin had been easier. This time was different. I returned to school exhausted, terribly homesick for the first time, and hopelessly behind in my most difficult class, organic chemistry.

After a few days back at school, I came down with the flu. I stayed in bed for three days, unable to eat, drink, or drag myself to the bathroom for a shower. I was dehydrated and depressed and beginning to panic about my classes.

Debbie insisted I go to the infirmary, where the doctor pronounced my blood sugar "through the roof." He treated me for two days with IV fluids, liquid nutrition, and extra insulin. I recovered and returned to class, sure that I was resilient enough to salvage the semester.

Except for my chemistry professor, who was strictly a lecturer and test-giver and who disregarded our questions as if we were waving our arms for exercise, my professors were understanding and willing to help me make up my work. Still, I couldn't get over the C I would be lucky to get in chemistry. The carbon and hydrogen diagrams on the lecture hall's overhead projector left me completely bewildered. I just sat there, pen in hand, not even knowing how to get it down on paper. My failure to grasp a subject so important to my degree made me think hard about the career choice I had made.

I had been planning to spend Thanksgiving on campus, but three days before the holiday, in the time it took me to walk from my room to the hallway telephone, I decided I was leaving school.

"Mom, I've decided to come home."

The line was quiet for several seconds. She was doing the math, I supposed, wondering how in the world they would pay for another flight so soon after my recent trip home.

Mom recovered and asked, "For the holiday?"

"No," I said. "For good. I just don't feel good."

I didn't know if that was the whole truth. My health was certainly not the only reason, but I couldn't put my finger on any one thing. That became apparent as I muddled through the required exit interviews with each of my professors. I told each a different story.

"I want to go back home and commute to Ohio State," I told my psychology professor. "I wasn't ready for a school that big when I started here, but now I think I am."

He leaned back in his chair, clasped his hands behind his head, and looked at me skeptically. "You're throwing away a sure A in a difficult class," he said. "The homesickness will go away, you know. Going home isn't always the cure."

"I know," I said, looking down at my lap. "I'm sorry, but I'm sure about this."

I wasn't sure about anything. My decision suddenly seemed irresponsible and immature. I had made it, though, so now I needed his signature on my exit form and I needed to go.

I told my French professor I had just learned I was diabetic and I didn't think I could manage it away from home. The first part of that was the most blatant lie I had ever told. The second part was as close to the truth as I had allowed myself to tread. She signed my paper quickly and wished me well.

The interview with my chemistry professor was cold and hurried. I said I was leaving because I was hopelessly lost in his class and wasn't sure any more if I was cut out for nursing.

He signed my form and looked up without expression. "Did you think it would be easy?"

"Yes, I guess I did."

I slid the paper from under his hand and went back to the dorm to pack.

Everyone in the dorm was packing to go somewhere that weekend, so I quietly joined in, beginning by folding my clothes into two green vinyl suitcases. When I put my sewing machine and typewriter into two boxes I had found in the basement, Debbie noticed.

"You hauling all of that to Janelle's room just for the weekend?"

Students staying on campus for the holiday had been asked to relocate for four days to one dorm. I had arranged to share a room in the dorm facing mine with a girl I worked with in the library.

"No," I said, folding together the flaps on the larger box. "I'm going home."

"Just for Thanksgiving, right?"

Debbie gave my pile of belongings a puzzled look. "You *are* coming back, aren't you?"

"No," I said, unable to look at her.

Debbie would be the one, I knew, who cared that I was not going to become a nurse. I had talked about staying in Texas after graduation, had said maybe she and I would even work together one day. But she was also the one who would understand why I was going. She didn't make me explain my decision, and I was grateful.

I sat in the window seat of the first row behind first class and gazed out at the carts of luggage rolling about on the tarmac. I thought this flight—home to Columbus by way of Chicago—would be the longest morning of my life. I thought about how I would explain my abrupt departure from school, although no one at home would push for an explanation if I didn't offer one.

The man who settled into the seat beside me engaged me quickly in conversation. His attire was well put together, but casual. Khakis with a crease, a salmon-colored button-down shirt, wire-rimmed glasses and suede loafers on sockless feet. Not an executive, I decided, but not a student either. Thirty, maybe.

"Going home for Thanksgiving break?" he asked.

I must have looked like a student. "Yes," I said, wanting to keep it simple. "You?"

"I've been in Dallas for a second interview. I don't think I'm getting the job, though. I'm going to New York now for Thanksgiving dinner at my mother's."

We talked casually as we headed toward Chicago, where we would each take a connecting flight. His mother, he said, would underbake the pumpkin pie, as usual, then dig out the gooey middle and fill the hole with whipped cream. The guests would ooh and aah over her beautiful creation. She would smile sweetly and say thank you.

My dad would swear at the turkey as he wrestled it with knife and fork. My Uncle Al, I explained, was our designated carver, but he would not be coming this year.

The young man and I talked about having seen Rod McKuen perform his poetry in Dallas. We had coincidentally been at the same concert on the same night. Did I think McKuen was a significant poet, or did women just think he was terribly romantic?

"Both," I said, remembering McKuen's soulful reading about his lost cat, Sloopy.

He turned and looked directly at me for the first time. "What's next for you?" He waited, and I could see it mattered to him. He had admitted that his own future was uncertain. Somehow he had sensed the same about mine.

And then, somewhere over Missouri, I told it all to this complete stranger.

"Well, I just abandoned a great scholarship at TCU. Three semesters into the nursing program, I just walked away. I don't know what's next for me."

"You must have had a good reason," he said, waiting for me to continue.

"I'm diabetic," I said quietly, "and I finally met my match. I didn't know how to handle it in that environment."

For the next half hour, I explained how the diabetic hurdles I had faced in the first ten years had just seemed like small assignments—pass or fail. And somehow, I had always passed. Until now, my problems—the cravings, the distasteful medical procedures, the peer pressure, my efforts to spare others the inconvenience of my disease—had only required some of my attention some of the time. Getting through the day-to-day without letting diabetes trip me up had allowed me to believe I was successfully managing it.

But I had finally landed in a place where I had to admit I couldn't do it all. Trying to do it all, pretending there was *nothing* in my way, had caused me my first real sickness from diabetes. It had scared me enough to make me leave behind the opportunity I had thought was the only road to success.

I looked over and realized I was giving this kind man an earful he hadn't bargained for, allowing him only an occasional *Hmm* or *Oh, really?*

He was still listening intently, but I changed gears and said, "My senior class voted me most likely to succeed. And now here I sit. Isn't life strange?"

I waited for him to tell me that yes, life certainly is strange, and I had better get used to it, and I should get myself back to school after Thanksgiving and give it another try.

But he said, "Oh, you'll be successful. It just won't look the way you thought it would. It may be different for you than for most."

I should have asked him how he knew. He probably had a story of his own to tell. But I chose to just believe him, and I thanked him. We were circling to land.

16

Our Thanksgiving was like all the others—football in the front yard, the Macy's parade on television, and lots and lots of food. If my parents were disappointed about my leaving school, they didn't let it show.

I settled in quietly. Mom and Dad had allowed Nancy to redecorate my room and move into it, so I unpacked my things in the rec room downstairs, where an extra set of bunk beds became my temporary bedroom. I planned to live at home only until I could find a job, buy a car, and rent a place of my own.

Schedules within our household had become less predictable while I was away, but Mom still cooked for those who were home at mealtime. That helped me get back on track, back to eating meat and bread, fruits and vegetables, on a more regular basis. I felt in control again.

After a week at home, I found a waitress job at Bill Knapp's Restaurant. A longtime favorite in Michigan, the chain was expanding to Ohio and was opening three restaurants in the Columbus area. Within a few months, my supervisor encouraged me to join Bill Knapp's management training program. I was enjoying my waitress job and making good money, but I welcomed the chance to do more.

My grandmother gave me Grandpa Curly's car. It had been sitting in her driveway undriven since October. Mom and Dad drove to Wisconsin to retrieve the 1963 Buick

LeSabre. It was a big, white tank of a car—not exactly a young girl's dream—but it started even on subzero mornings and glided easily over snowy Columbus roads as I went to and from work that winter.

When I learned I was being assigned to the newest Bill Knapp's restaurant under construction on the far east side of Columbus, I rented a room in an old brick house just east of downtown, in a community called Bexley. I shared the house with three other young women, one of whom had inherited the house from her parents.

I reconnected with Barry, the ice cream factory guy, spending much of my off time at the house near Ohio State University where he rented a room. His roommates—a Bill and a Brad, two Judys and a Paul—were more sociable than mine, so we spent little time at my place.

Barry and I married on Thanksgiving weekend the following fall. Getting engaged in late summer had seemed like the right thing to do, and planning a wedding was exciting, but nothing felt right on the day I walked down the aisle on my father's arm. I almost turned back.

By the time Barry and I had properly set up housekeeping and acquired a second car and a dog, we were bored with it all, and with each other. I might have stayed in that marriage indefinitely, assuming that married life is sometimes just boring, had I not met Mick.

I wasn't thinking about divorce when Mick entered my life, but after knowing him for just a few weeks, I could think of nothing else. Barry and I filed for a no-fault divorce in June of 1975, dividing without argument the few possessions we had accumulated in a year and a half. Mick and I married three weeks after my divorce became final, on July 14, 1975.

Mick knew nothing about diabetes when we married. He learned about it on a need-to-know basis as we began almost immediately to deal with its complications.

In early spring of 1977, just before I turned twenty-four, I was driving home from work one night and took the wrong exit. I looked up at the green exit sign over the highway, and it looked like the lettering had been erased. Only the sign's white border was clear to me. I took the exit anyway, hoping it was the one I had used dozens of times before, but I was miles from where I should have been. I knew my way home from there by city streets, but the headlights I met on that congested four-lane road were askew and doubled. I slowed to a crawl and concentrated on staying in my own lane. I arrived home in a panic and in tears.

My vision had been blurry for several days. At work, the numbers on the cash register seemed misshapen; I thought my eyes were tired. The dining room seemed darker than usual; I thought someone had gone too far with the dimmer. But I hadn't been alarmed until that night on the highway. I blamed the Tylenol with codeine I was taking for back pain. Diabetic neuropathy, a condition caused by nerve damage, was the source of my pain. All other treatments had failed, so I continued taking the medication, assuming the vision problem would end when my prescription did. Although blurry vision can be a side effect of codeine, my problem was more serious than that, and more permanent. In just one evening, diabetic retinopathy—broken blood vessels in the backs of my eyes—had caused me to become legally blind.

I underwent a series of laser treatments intended to stop the tiny blood vessels from continuing to leak. Eyes wide open, pupils dilated, and with instructions not to move a muscle, I sat for thirty minutes at a time and stared into an uncomfortably intense light as hundreds of consecutive laser shots targeted the offending vessels. After six weekly laser sessions, we waited for results and hoped for the best.

The best was the news that although we had probably arrested the disease for some unknown period of time, my vision had not improved.

"In fact," the doctor said, "your vision has deteriorated even further. We may not have caught this in time. Let's let things settle down a little and take another look in a few months."

So home I went to learn how to live in a shadowy world, thinking that of course I would be working again as soon as this problem cleared up. It didn't take long for me to realize that would never happen. Mick and I accepted that we would now be living on one income. I didn't know how we'd manage. We trimmed our budget, and I set out to become an efficient and enthusiastic homemaker.

It was in quiet protest that Mick and I painted our bedroom bright robin's-egg blue, our bathroom deep orange, and our living room seagrass green. I would begin my recovery by not living within white walls gone gray.

During those first few weeks, there were occasional moments when I imagined my surroundings looked a shade brighter, the outlines of objects slightly more defined. In reality I was just finding my way around more easily each day, bumping into furniture and tripping over rugs less often. I was learning that doorways were narrower than they appeared, that tabletop corners were sharper, appliance knobs more left or right than where my eyes guided my hand. And Mick finally convinced me that the pictures on the walls did not all need straightening.

I learned too that you don't figure out all at once how to do everyday tasks with limited vision. You decide one day that it would be fun to bake cookies again. You find a way to do it. Early on, you learn that if you don't use a dark-colored measuring cup to measure milk, you will, at least once, pour two cups of milk into a one-cup measure and not realize it until the excess runs off the counter's edge onto your shoes. Then a few days later, when there's not enough milk for morning cereal, and you don't know the new neighbors well enough yet to borrow basic supplies, you get brave enough to take the bus to the grocery store. This requires saying out loud for the first time to a complete stranger—a grumpy-looking bus driver—that you'll need help crossing the street when he folds open his door at the stop you think is across from the shopping center.

And so it went. Each new desire required mastering a half-dozen smaller assignments. Each accomplishment emerged from the rubble of countless mistakes. Every little thing took forever. My life was busier than it had ever been, but I just smiled when well-meaning friends asked how I was managing to fill my days.

We filled our days with work and friends and music, a kitten and a puppy. Our house became the gathering place for parties, card games, and home-cooked dinners for our bachelor friends.

In a short time, Mick learned what I was and was not able to do around the house. He would watch me struggle with a chore for a reasonable length of time, knowing I preferred to handle as many of my usual responsibilities as possible. If I gave up in frustration, then the task became his, and he gladly took it on.

Many household chores required a team effort. I learned that with 8X reading glasses, I could guide needle and thread through a button's holes and reattach it to a shirt cuff, but first I needed Mick to thread the needle for me and choose the right size and color button from my sewing box. If I dropped the button or the needle came unthreaded, we were back to square one. I could balance the checkbook with a magnifier if Mick first sorted the canceled checks by number. I cooked and served gourmet dinners on special occasions, but the candle-lighting waited until he arrived at the table.

If I had been single when I lost my vision, it might have been cause for despair, the tragedy everyone else thought it was when they heard the news. But we were still newlyweds and still learning about each other in general, having been married less than two years at this first sign of diabetic complications. Adding new layers of compromise to a life we were still creating together just seemed like part of the plan.

There were, of course, days when I felt helpless and frustrated. When two men arrived one day to replace the carpet in our living room and hallway, I stayed in the bedroom out of their way. At lunchtime, one of them shouted toward the bedroom, "We're going out to the truck to have our lunch. Back in a half hour."

I headed down the hall toward the kitchen to fix myself a sandwich. I didn't know they had removed the register from the hallway floor. They didn't know I couldn't see all the way to my feet. Just outside the kitchen doorway, I stepped into the hole. Only my behind and a bend in the duct kept me from sliding all the way to the basement. I sat on the edge of the opening, legs dangling, and wasted every obscenity I knew on an empty house. And then I sat there and sobbed until there was nothing left.

Feeling sorry for myself wasn't a luxury I allowed often. I had so much to learn and relearn, and I was grateful for the vision I still had. The most difficult part was learning to tell people how much or how little help I needed.

Mick had a natural sense for how to guide me without a lot of fuss. When I needed to step up onto a sidewalk, he would quietly say, "Curb," and offer me his arm. Or he would place my hand on a handrail and announce, "Four steps down and then a landing." Without comment, he moved what stood in my way, picked up what I dropped, and wiped up my spills.

Others who ventured out with me had a harder time understanding what I could and could not see. Sometimes a friend would grip my arm tightly all through the grocery store as if I couldn't steer clear of the shelves, and yet she would seem surprised when I mistook a can of Alpo for a can of Spaghetti-O's.

I was reluctant at first to tell anyone up front that too much help was as likely to cause me to stumble as too little. But after pushing a shopping cart full of groceries over a curb one day and watching a week's worth of food roll all over the parking lot, I swallowed my pride and became more direct about describing my vision in advance to anyone offering to help me with errands.

"This is how I see," I explained. "Imagine you've put together a jigsaw puzzle on a dark table. Now pull apart some large sections just a little so the puzzle is no longer exactly square. Turn a few pieces over, gray side up, and remove a few altogether. Now lay a piece of wax paper over the whole thing and dim the lights. That's what the landscape looks like to me."

Then they would get it. A little crooked, a little cloudy, some details fuzzy, some completely gone.

I learned to identify people not by their name tags, but by their shapes and hair color and the sound of their voices. I recognized buildings only because they stood where they had always stood.

I did mourn my inability to read entire books, but I soon learned how to navigate short passages of normal-size print with a handheld, lighted magnifier. With some central vision in my left eye and limited peripheral vision in my right, I learned to close the left eye for distance and the right for reading. It was slow going, but I needed to be able to read books not available on tape if they were important to me. I devised ways to do what mattered most. That list continues to grow.

17

In 1978, after two of the coldest Ohio winters in decades, Mick and I decided, on a whim, to move to a warmer climate. He would leave behind the restaurant management job he didn't love any more.

We went to The Little Professor book store and chose Greensboro, North Carolina from a travel book. We liked its weather statistics and its proximity to both the mountains and the ocean.

Greensboro lacked adequate public transportation, but otherwise it was everything our research had promised. We found housing within a few blocks of a grocery store, bank, drug store and post office. I became an avid walker, my ever-widening circle of destinations providing the exercise I needed for better blood sugar control.

Eventually, though, I began to have problems with my feet—blisters becoming infected ulcers, slow to heal and aggravated by the poor circulation of diabetes.

A year after our move, on a particularly beautiful morning, I decided to venture out to Four Seasons Mall. It was more than a mile uphill from our apartment, and I didn't really need to buy anything, but a mall shopping trip was something I hadn't attempted since my vision loss. I decided to go early, study the spring arrivals at the fabric store and have lunch at the mall, then buy a few groceries and head home.

I spent the whole day at the mall, becoming more brave at every corridor, exhilarated by my independence and not wanting the feeling to end. I left the mall without any packages, congratulating myself all the way home for my victories—two traffic lights, a busy parking lot, elevators, escalators, and a balcony café. I envisioned all the places I would go, now that I had conquered the mall.

Three days later, I noticed tiny blood spots on the rug outside the shower. The drops led to the doorway and down the hall, ending at the side of the bed, where I had dressed earlier in the day. I sat on the bed and studied the bottoms of my feet with my hands. On my right foot, I felt a rough spot just behind my fourth and fifth toes. Applying pressure caused no pain. Blotting with a tissue produced no blood. I applied antibiotic ointment from a tube and attached a small Band-Aid. On the second day, I saw drainage on the bandage and a yellowish spot on my sock. I soaked my foot in soapy water and redressed it. Still no pain.

But on the third day, my entire foot had become red and swollen. I couldn't get my tennis shoe on, and my entire calf was tender when I touched it. The knot on the bottom of my foot had grown to the size of a large marble. It felt spongy and warm when I pressed it.

I couldn't reach Mick at work, so I called a friend and asked her to take me to see my doctor. Robin hurried over and helped me down the stairs from our third floor apartment. With only a sock on my right foot, I gripped the railing with one hand, Robin's arm with the other, and hopped down to ground level.

Dr. Keller's nurse led me down the hall to an examining room. I sat on a paper-lined table, and she pulled out a foot rest so I could elevate my feet. My right foot and calf were throbbing now, and this new position brought some relief.

"Your temperature is 102," she announced, removing a thermometer from under my tongue.

She carefully slipped the sock from my foot and peeled away the bandage. "Oh dear," she said, draping a small white towel over my foot and hurrying from the room.

"I hear your foot's in trouble," Dr. Keller said cheerfully as he entered the room. With thumb and forefinger, like a magician with a trick handkerchief, he whisked away the towel. His face suddenly grim, he asked, "How did this happen?"

"I don't know. I didn't notice the sore until I saw blood spots on the bath mat. It didn't hurt, and for a few days it seemed to be healing."

Dr. Keller pressed the ball of my foot, then my ankle and finally, the back of my calf just below my knee. He showed me a red line running up the inside of my leg. As he ran his thumb along the vein, I felt pain for the first time, a sharp pain that made me jump.

"The red streak means you have an infection that has traveled into the bloodstream. I need to admit you and get you started on IV antibiotics right away."

I couldn't believe my ears. "The *hospital?*" I said, my voice too loud for the tiny room. "It was a blister the size of a dime!"

"It probably started out that way," Dr. Keller explained, "but then it healed only on the surface and allowed the infection to push deep into your foot. A normal person wouldn't walk around on a foot this infected, but diabetes makes your foot numb to it, so you carried on as usual." He wrapped a gauze bandage loosely around my foot. "Who's here with you today?"

"My friend Robin is in the waiting room. She has to get on to work, but she could probably drop me off at home to pack a few things. My husband will be home at five, so he could take me to the hospital then."

I realized how serious my condition was when the doctor insisted I go directly to Wesley Long Hospital. "It's less than five minutes from here. Your husband can bring anything you need later tonight."

Mick arrived at the hospital just after Robin and I reached the admissions office. He thanked her for her help, and she went on her way. The next few hours were so hectic, we found only brief uninterrupted moments to discuss what was happening.

"That blister got this bad overnight?" Mick asked, confused by all the urgent activity in my room.

"It did," I said. "I knew it when I tried to put on my shoe this morning."

When visiting hours ended, Mick went home to sleep, but sleep was impossible for me. I lay awake trying to comprehend how a tiny sore of unknown cause could become such an emergency.

For the next twelve hours, nurses and technicians tiptoed around my room in the half-dark, drawing blood, changing IV fluids, administering Tylenol for my fever, injecting my insulin, and concocting alternating foot baths of warm peroxide and diluted Betadine.

The next day, when Dr. Keller made his morning rounds, he unwound the bandage from my foot and breathed an audible sigh.

"I think we got lucky," he said with a relieved smile.

I realized then that my foot had been in serious trouble, that he had expected I might lose it—or part of it—had we not treated it in time.

I had paid attention for fifteen years to all the warnings about vigilant foot care, foot infections, and amputation. *Examine your feet every day. Don't walk outside barefoot. Get immediate treatment for any sore that doesn't heal.*

I had listened attentively and given these warnings medium weight, like other cautionary advice about things like seeing a dentist at the first sign of tooth pain or prying loose a tick before it burrows too deep. Watching the look now on Dr. Keller's face as he realized my toes were returning from blue-gray to rosy pink, I felt a little queasy envisioning the unthinkable outcome we had avoided.

For my remaining two days in the hospital, I still feared my foot would take a turn for the worse, but on the third day, toes intact and swelling gone, Dr. Keller released me to the care of a podiatrist.

"See Dr. Weisberger before the end of the week," Dr. Keller advised as he signed my referral. "Don't let time get away from you."

I visited Dr. Weisberger's office twice weekly for the next two months. He was an elderly man with a patient, grandfatherly voice.

"This condition is what I see most often in diabetics. Any little thing can cause it," he assured me, "and it sure can get away from you in a hurry."

He described for me some of the diabetic cases he had treated: a man who had stepped on the broken tip of a sewing machine needle and not known it until his entire leg had become inflamed, a woman who had walked all day at work wearing a shoe with a tiny cat toy wedged in its toe, and a tennis player who had played three sets wearing snug shoes over a wrinkled sock.

The doctor and I surmised that my trek to the mall the previous week in open-toed sandals had probably caused my foot ulcer—an unusual pressure spot in a shoe I hadn't worn before or a tiny pebble or twig finding its way between my exposed toes.

"Diabetic neuropathy," Dr. Weisberger explained, "doesn't cause such injuries, but when they do occur, the nerve damage keeps diabetics from feeling pain that would keep most people off their feet."

The miscommunication between the nerves in my feet and my brain had allowed me to keep walking.

At each visit, Dr. Weisberger reopened the wound, scraped away the unhealthy tissue that seemed determined to crowd out healthy healing, then photographed and measured the wound and redressed it. With each visit—I thought they would never end—the newly trimmed ulcer measured a fraction of a centimeter smaller.

I finally healed, vowing never to go barefoot or wear sandals again. I toured my feet with my hands every morning, searching for bumps or abrasions. I reached inside my shoes to make sure nothing stray had landed in them. Blisters, calluses and ulcers recurred over the years, but I sought medical attention promptly at the first sign of trouble.

I first heard about home blood sugar monitors in 1984. We were still living in Greensboro, and I had just turned thirty-one. Thinking it was exactly what I needed, I asked Dr. Keller about getting one. He discouraged the idea.

"The machines are expensive and they're not covered yet by most insurance plans. The test strips add another big expense."

Not willing to accept that the cost would be impossible, I waited for him to continue. "Besides," he went on, "patients tend to obsess about their blood sugar levels when they can test at home all day long."

Obsessing a little about my blood sugar might be a good idea, I thought, but this doctor was not going to help me do it.

I talked to my pharmacist, who agreed to bend the rules for me. Without a prescription from my doctor, he rented me a new monitor for a small monthly fee. Eighteen months later, when I had paid the total price of $840, he considered it mine. The machine was a dinosaur compared to today's sleek, hand-held devices, but it gave me better control than I had ever managed before. I could finally see how every calorie I consumed and every calorie I burned affected my blood sugar.

Eventually, more sophisticated machines, a wider range of insulin choices, and a growing belief that patients were capable of tweaking their own insulin routines, made portable monitors indispensable among diabetics. At the time, though, I relied on mine only to help me control my food intake—no small feat, given my past struggles with diet.

18

After ten years in Greensboro, we had begun to consider it home. I loved its mild, beautifully distinct seasons—Wisconsin without frostbite, Ohio with a breeze. We might have stayed there beyond retirement, had it not been for a job offer too good to turn down.

In 1989, Mick accepted a position as finance director at a new Atlanta Pontiac dealership. We rented an old brick house in Fayetteville, a town just south of the city. It was an easy commute for Mick, but it turned out to be a poor choice for me. It lacked both public transportation and pedestrian-friendly streets. After a year, we moved to Peachtree City, a few miles closer to Atlanta. We chose this community because Mick was sure I'd be able to navigate its eighty miles of paved trails by golf cart, a favorite mode of transportation for Peachtree City residents. I didn't know whether I could do that or not, but Mick took a leap of faith and bought me a used golf cart.

We took turns behind the wheel the first time, easing down the street and onto the trail, around the golf course, through the woods to the Kroger store.

The next morning, Mick parked the golf cart at the end of the driveway, facing the street, and went off to work.

"I'm not going to drive that thing by myself," I said as he handed me the key. "I'll get lost, and no one will even know to look for me."

He smiled. "Do what you want."

By noon, the grocery store was calling my name. I ventured out, clutching the wheel, creeping along, hugging my edge of the trail. I trusted all the other drivers would stay right of center.

Driving was a privilege I had never dreamed of regaining. For fourteen years, I had relied on friends, family, and Mick to get me where I needed to go, sometimes feeling I was creating a major inconvenience with my minor missions. Now buying a greeting card at Hallmark, getting a haircut, and cashing a check at the bank's drive-through would be solo excursions for me.

Sometimes when I had no particular destination, I just drove. I stretched my comfort zone occasionally by taking an unfamiliar trail just to see where it would go. Each trail sprouted several others. Every wrong turn revealed a new neighborhood, a new bridge or tunnel, a new way home.

This newfound freedom introduced me to all kinds of dangerous food temptations, at a time when I had finally negotiated a reasonable peace with my diabetes management. Despite its small population—just over 19,000—Peachtree City boasted an abundance of grocery stores, food specialty shops, and restaurants. I could reach them all by golf cart.

But getting out of the house every day eliminated some of my usual reasons for overeating. I no longer reached for food out of boredom. I didn't stir up a batch of cookies just because I was stuck at home on Mick's longest work days. And by some miracle, my lifelong love affair with chocolate was waning. So when I drove, I took in the peaceful scenery and bypassed all but the essential food places.

Mick and I knew immediately that Peachtree City was ideal for us. For as long as I could drive the golf cart, this would be home. We couldn't imagine anything anywhere luring us from this place where I could drive. We started shopping casually for a house to buy. The one we were renting was for sale, but its location on Braelinn Golf Course added $20,000 to a price that would otherwise have fit our budget.

So we drove around on our golf cart on Sundays to become familiar with other neighborhoods and the ease with which I could get from those neighborhoods to my favorite destinations. Plans for serious house-shopping with a realtor came to a halt that September, everything suddenly on hold, when my primary care physician, Dr. Warner, suggested during my annual physical that I should see a kidney specialist. My kidney function had declined significantly, she said, since my last visit.

Previous doctors had warned me about diabetic nephropathy, a disease caused by damage to the microscopic blood vessels supplying the kidneys. Until now, it had always been a concern that came and went, like those gray clouds that hover briefly overhead and then drift away without changing the day's plans.

It took me a few weeks to make an appointment with the specialist Dr. Warner had recommended. No big hurry. I thought I knew what Dr. Fulton would offer—advice about prolonging kidney function with diet and good blood sugar control.

Finally, I sat one afternoon on the end of an examining table and heard the bad news. Dr. Fulton had received and reviewed my recent lab reports. My kidney function was down to a level that required immediate and aggressive treatment. After he explained to me the significance of the numbers on the page, he got right to the point. "This condition is irreversible. Transplant or dialysis. Those are our options."

I was struck dumb with disbelief. I sat there motionless, unable to speak, eyes wide open like an eight-year-old watching his new baseball roll into a storm drain. *What do you mean there's no getting it back?*

Realizing I was not likely to absorb further information at that moment, Dr. Fulton did what experienced bearers of bad news do; he left the room to allow me to cry. "I'll give you a few minutes alone."

I thought he stayed away an awfully long time, considering how few tears I actually shed before pulling myself together and gathering a little anger. He finally returned, quietly pulled a chair up in front of me, and asked, "Are you afraid?"

I remember thinking he must have a daughter of his own. The sadness and genuine concern in his voice was not bedside manner learned in medical school.

"First of all," I started, "let's scratch dialysis off the list. It's not going to happen. It's the only thing I've ever really been afraid of."

I knew very little about dialysis, but the thought of it had always troubled me. I certainly had some misconceptions about it. I thought it only happened to old people. I considered it the end of the road and a terrible way to go.

I had shared a hospital room once with a woman on dialysis. She was always thirsty, her mouth so dry it was hard for her to form words. She often asked for water, but her fluid intake was severely limited because of her dialysis.

When the woman's husband arrived one morning for a visit, she told him, "The nurse brought me my water, but I spilled most of it. Would you go and fill this?"

He quizzed her about how much she thought she had spilled.

"Almost all," she said. "I only got one sip."

He looked at the empty paper cup and down at the floor. Then he glanced over at me and I could tell he had been through this before. I had seen the nurse bring the water, had heard no fuss over a spill. I thought how sad it must be to feel so thirsty you would manipulate people for an extra three ounces of water. I knew how she felt. She didn't want to break the rules; she wanted water. It reminded me of times when I had imagined my blood sugar felt low so I could justify having a glass of juice or a piece of hard candy. The threat of a low blood sugar reaction was the only legitimate reason to eat something intensely sweet. I wondered how I would do if I had to add a water restriction to a diet I already found difficult.

Dr. Fulton smiled at my reaction to the dialysis idea. He seemed pleased that by default I had landed on the treatment he had already chosen for me. He told me I was an ideal candidate for transplant, young enough and healthy enough to withstand the surgery, competent enough to manage the complexities of transplant maintenance.

I was feeling more in control again, now that we had removed the dialysis card from the table. Now we could move on.

I was sure the doctor would welcome some good news I had learned a few months earlier, before I had any idea I would need it. My dad had called one day that summer and told me about an article he had just read in the Columbus Dispatch. Ohio State University had been doing a new procedure—simultaneous transplants of kidney and pancreas. Their program was limited to Type One diabetics in need of a kidney and also suffering from additional diabetic complications. Several dozen dual transplants had already been successfully performed, and I fit the profile, so I thought the option was worth exploring.

Dr. Fulton disagreed. He was familiar with OSU's work with pancreas transplants and with other similar programs. He told me, "Nine out of ten patients wish they hadn't chosen the procedure. They're having some problems."

"What kind of problems?" I asked, hoping he wasn't just going to leave it at that.

"All *kinds* of problems," he said in a voice that was suddenly impatient.

I hoped he was just behind on his research, but I didn't know enough yet myself to disagree. So we sat for a moment and looked at each other.

I wanted Dr. Fulton to set aside my immediate problem—kidney failure—and to hear what had brought me to this point. Twenty-seven years of diabetes. A lifetime just wanting it to go away and not caring how. That was a long story, though, and I didn't expect him to have time for it.

He looked at his watch. "Is your husband with you today?" He glanced at my chart. "It's Michael, right?"

"It's Mick. And no, he's not with me. A friend drove me today."

I hadn't come to this appointment expecting such bad news it would require a family conference.

The drive from Atlanta's far north side to the far south was an hour and a half in heavy late-afternoon traffic.

"How was your appointment?" Linda asked.

"Fine," I said, "but I may need a kidney transplant."

"Oh really?" she asked absently, weaving lane-changers requiring all of her attention.

We were one exit from home when she asked, "Do you mind if I make a quick stop at the mall?"

"Of course not," I lied.

I did mind very much. I had been trying without much success to keep it all together for just ten more miles. I sat captive in the car for an hour at the mall, wondering why it was urgent that she have a leather wallet monogrammed in September, a gift her husband wouldn't open until Christmas.

I was angry at all the wrong people—my dear friend, who had given up her whole day for me, and all the shoppers in the mall parking lot, planning already for Christmas. I didn't know if I could plan anything at all.

I was angry, too, at the kind, conscientious doctor who could not encourage my reckless optimism—my willingness to be rid of diabetes at any cost.

19

Never before had I felt so hopeless I just wanted to give up. It was a foreign feeling for me that day when I came into my house, curled up in my recliner, and had a complete meltdown. The cat wanted out. The message light was flashing on the phone. The morning's laundry lay wet in the washer, breakfast dishes in the kitchen sink. And I could not move.

I couldn't even remember how late Mick was scheduled to work that night. Probably nine o'clock, since it was already past six. I wouldn't call him at work with this kind of news. His office was rarely empty long enough for even a brief private conversation.

I also decided not to call my parents just yet. Maybe tomorrow, when I had come to terms with the news myself. Dad would want details I didn't have yet. Mom would ask what they could do to help. I would hear the helplessness in her voice and I would lose it all over again. They were 600 miles away, still living near Columbus, where Mick and I had left them and all of my siblings when we started our migration south. I didn't think anyone could help from so far away.

I dialed my sister Nancy. I knew she would be home, and I knew she wouldn't overreact. She listened to my news quietly. I heard tears in her voice for just a minute before she got right down to business. "So what's next?" she asked, as if we were mapping out a shopping plan. "You'll need a donor, right? How do we find out how many of us can do that?"

"I only need one kidney," I said, and we both laughed. I hadn't thought about a donor at all. It was too much to think about now. But the way Nancy kept using the words *we* and *us* assured me that when it was time, I wouldn't be alone.

We hung up, and I headed for the shower. I stood under extra-hot water until it finally ran cold, my fatigue and anger and tears down the drain.

By the time Mick got home, I had regained my composure to some degree. He shed his tie and stepped out of his shoes, but he returned to the living room when he realized I hadn't followed him to the bedroom to chatter at him about his day and mine.

I must not have looked as refreshed as I thought. He saw that I was struggling not to cry. He put his arms around me and asked, "What happened today?" He waited while I came up with the words to tell him the future we had planned was sliding off the edge.

I don't remember all of what I said. I repeated the diagnosis and the options I had heard from my doctor, but I didn't share with Mick the real fear I had felt all evening. *I wouldn't blame you if you didn't want to go through this with me, if you couldn't deal with all of this for even one more day.*

I knew how hurt and helpless he would feel if I even implied he would ever bail out on me. In our fifteen years of marriage, he had accommodated more medical disasters than most young husbands ever have to. He had learned about diabetes as each of my complications had occurred. Now his reaction was the same as always. "What do you need me to do?"

What we needed to do seemed more clear the next morning after a good night's sleep and our regular morning routine, a cup of coffee in front of the Today Show. Mick asked, "What about that procedure they're doing in Ohio? The one your dad read about?"

Before falling asleep the night before, I had thought briefly about the kidney and pancreas idea. I had set it aside in the name of sleep. Feeling less exhausted now, and more optimistic, it seemed I should at least look into it as Plan B. I would give Dr. Fulton the benefit of the doubt—admit he had erred, if at all, on the side of caution and with my best interest at heart.

But although I was willing to be a cooperative, compliant patient, I would not be an uninformed one. As soon as Mick left for work, his question about OSU's program still hanging in the air, I gathered notebook and pen and settled into a chair next to the phone.

I called Mom first. Nancy had given her my news by the time I reached her. I had asked her to do that, not knowing when I would feel up to calling.

"I was going to give you another hour and then call you," Mom said when our call connected. I could tell it had worried her to wait. We talked only long enough for me to tell her Dr. Fulton's diagnosis and recommendation—a kidney transplant at an Atlanta hospital. Mom told me she was quite sure she and I were the same blood type—A, and that she was willing—determined, in fact—to be my donor.

Mom was sixty-one years old. I didn't know at the time that her age was six years beyond the maximum for donors. In 1990, kidney donation was major surgery, the recovery for donors much more difficult than for recipients. When I did learn about the age restriction, I told Mom, "They won't consider anyone over fifty-five as a donor."

"I'll lie then," she said. Lying was a rare sin for my mother, but I knew she meant it.

Within a few days, all of my siblings had learned or verified their blood types. All were Type A. Two were, and two were not, in excellent health, but all four were willing to donate. Only my dad had an incompatible blood type. He would not be a donor possibility.

Before ending our call, I told Mom, "I'm going to get some information from Ohio State about their transplant program. Maybe I'll know more by the end of the week. I'll try to call you on Friday."

"We'll wait to hear from you," she said. "Dad will be home then. He'll want to talk to you."

A few minutes later, I was surprised how quickly my call to OSU Medical Center was routed to the transplant department. Expecting to hear *We'll be glad to mail you some information*, I was pleased to find a nurse at the end of the line eager to answer my questions.

"I understand you're doing pancreas transplants in diabetics," I said.

"We are," she said. "Right now the procedure is reserved for patients who already need a kidney. Have you been told you have end stage renal failure?"

"Not in those words," I replied. "But my nephrologist told me yesterday that my kidneys are failing. I'll need dialysis soon, or a transplant."

"What we need to do first," she said, "is to see your most recent lab reports. If your creatinine level has reached 3.9 or higher, we go from there and consider you for a kidney transplant. Then we will determine if a pancreas transplant would also benefit you."

Creatinine is a metabolic waste product normally cleared from the bloodstream by the kidneys. Its level in the bloodstream rises as kidney function declines. I assumed mine was significantly elevated, but could not remember having heard a specific number. I agreed to have my lab reports sent.

I avoided asking Dr. Fulton. Although I didn't dare burn that bridge prematurely, I had a feeling I wouldn't be seeing him again. I would ask my internist, Dr. Warner, if she could provide OSU a copy.

Dr. Warner agreed she would send whatever OSU requested, but when I told her why I was consulting the transplant department at a hospital so far away, her reaction was hesitant.

"I haven't read much lately about the success of pancreas transplants. You know they're still considered experimental, right?"

"I know that," I said.

She continued. "Sometimes with experimental procedures, teaching hospitals have more to gain than patients do."

I respected Dr. Warner's opinion—she is still my doctor today—but even after hearing this same cautionary advice from two doctors, I could not let go. I would look into it further. I wanted to hear what I wanted to hear.

I called my uncle, Herb Sandmire, a well-known physician in Green Bay. As a child, I had spent summer vacation time with him, my aunt Crystal, and their five children. The youngest of these cousins, David, had been diagnosed with Type One diabetes as a young adult. I knew that a doctor with a diabetic son would lend a caring and thoughtful perspective to my decision.

I told Uncle Herb about Dr. Fulton's warning regarding unhappy pancreas recipients. I mentioned Dr. Warner's opinion about research programs at university hospitals.

"So what do you think?" I prompted.

He thought for a long moment, my call and my question obviously having caught him off guard. He answered carefully. "I think maybe they're misinformed."

We discussed what he had recently studied about simultaneous kidney and pancreas transplants. They had been performed with acceptable success at a few universities around the country. Others were joining in the research and studying the procedure. The list of participating hospitals was growing. Many patients were doing well, although the longevity of pancreas transplants was yet to be determined.

The conservative optimism in my uncle's words allowed me to dismiss the advice of the others. That was all I needed.

When my lab reports had reached OSU, the transplant coordinator scheduled an appointment for me. It was early October already, and my appointment was for October 25 and 26. Everything was moving more quickly than I had expected. I had heard stories, though, about long, uncertain waits for organ transplants. I expected that after these preliminaries were over, I would join those hopeful patients who might or might not be able to wait it out.

Mick had planned to be with me for my orientation and prescreening appointments, but our plans changed when

Nancy's husband died suddenly on October 16. He had been admitted to the hospital with congestive heart failure after a long struggle with emphysema. When Nancy called to tell me Joe's condition was critical, that the doctor had said he wouldn't survive the night, I put a change of clothes and a toothbrush in a bag and arranged a ride to the airport. I reached Columbus an hour after Joe died. My brother Dennis picked me up at the airport and we went directly to my parents' house, where the rest of our family was already gathering.

Mick and I discussed by phone whether I would return home after the funeral and reschedule my OSU appointment. I was tempted to put it off until after the holidays. It would be a rough winter for Nancy, for her stepchildren, and for our family. It seemed inappropriate to be thinking about anything else.

But everyone, Nancy included, encouraged me not to change my plans. I decided to spend the week with my family and keep my appointment. Mick agreed. There would likely be future visits where his presence would be important. We needed to consider how many more trips we would make to Columbus in the coming months, how expensive that might become, and how often he could be away from his job.

On Wednesday, October 25, Dad and I went to an orientation meeting at the hospital. We sat in a conference room just large enough for a table and eight chairs. Four adults sat on each side of the narrow table. A man who looked too young to have the title *transplant coordinator* stood at the head of the table. We all made small talk while he sorted papers and answered phone messages.

A thin, pale woman, accompanied by her sister, said her kidney failure was due to a hereditary kidney disease. A young man whose wiry white hair belied his forty-something age explained he was hoping for a second kidney transplant. His first had failed after several years. I resisted asking how many.

Dad and I sat across from a couple who arrived late, apologizing for having stopped downstairs for popcorn and soft drinks. The woman offered her snacks around the table. We all declined. Extremely overweight and out of breath, she couldn't get comfortable in her chair. Although the coordinator hadn't yet introduced himself or acknowledged the group, in a very loud voice the woman asked, "What do you suppose made my kidney just blow up thattaway?"

I assumed she was a second-timer too, but we would not hear those details. The coordinator quickly asked for our attention.

I looked around at the others and thought I seemed in relatively good shape, too healthy to be among them. Maybe I was here prematurely. Maybe I could tolerate dialysis for a while. Probably everyone else in the room was enduring it. Maybe I could go on living with diabetes too. After all, no one had ever led me to believe it would be otherwise.

I remembered Dr. Fulton's warning that many pancreas transplant recipients ended up regretting their decision. I hadn't asked him why. Now I wanted to know, but I was the only patient in the group considering a dual transplant, so I didn't ask questions that applied only to me. I would save those for my interview with the transplant surgeon assigned to see me the following day. Today's meeting was about preliminary testing, waiting list procedure, and insurance. The coordinator gave brief, polite answers to a few dozen routine questions while handing out questionnaires, medical history forms, and preprinted orders for labwork. He thanked us then for coming and wished us well.

Dad and I left the orientation session and made a brief stop at the outpatient lab. A technician coaxed a half dozen tubes of blood from my uncooperative vein. He explained the need for so much blood: tests for the usual blood sugar, cholesterol, and electrolytes; tests for antibodies or excessive white blood cells, a sign of exposure to infection; initial studies of genetic markers to be matched with those of a donor.

My final stop for the day was at the hospital's cardiology lab, where I pedaled a stationary bike for fifteen minutes while a technician watched my heartbeat draw jagged lines on a glowing screen.

I could tell that my heart, which had not yet become a health issue, was passing the test. I would not allow myself to worry any more about failed transplants, about patients who were poor surgical risks, those who had just had bad luck, and those who would likely repeat past mistakes after getting a second chance. I vowed not to become one of those.

Dad and I returned to the hospital again the next day. We sat just inside the doorway of a bare little room—a makeshift office on a busy corridor—and waited. A tall, fair-haired doctor arrived wearing khakis and a light blue shirt. His lack of white jacket and stethoscope put me at ease. He sat briefly at a counter across from us and glanced at the front of a folder.

"I'm Dr. Tesi," he said, standing to shake my father's hand and then mine. "Carol Wilson?"

"Yes. And this is my dad, Dan Ward."

"What brings you all the way from Georgia to OSU?" he asked as he leafed through my file.

Before responding, I remembered the cassette recorder I had brought in my tote bag. I pulled it out and placed it on the counter next to the doctor. "Would it be okay if I recorded our conversation? My husband couldn't be here today."

Dr. Tesi reached over and plugged in the recorder, then pushed the *record* button.

I answered his question. "My family lives here. I lived here until I was twenty-six, and then my husband and I moved away. I don't drive any more, because I'm legally blind, so it's almost as easy for me to get to the Atlanta airport and fly here as to get a ride to north Atlanta where the good hospitals are. If I had surgery here, I could recover with my family, and my husband could get right back to his job."

Dr. Tesi considered this for a moment and nodded.

"Is it a problem that I live out of state?" I asked.

He abandoned the paperwork. "It could be," he said. "For a few reasons. The cost is one. The distance is another. I see that Medicare is your only insurance. They'll cover a kidney transplant as they would any other surgery. The pancreas is done at the same time, so some surgical and hospital expenses are charged only once. But any cost related only to the pancreas—procurement of the organ, for example— would be your responsibility. Medicare still considers pancreas transplants experimental."

My heart sank. I didn't know if he was talking about thousands of dollars or tens of thousands.

My father, almost silent until now, asked the question, "How much?"

"We ask that you be prepared to pay five thousand dollars when you're discharged," Dr. Tesi answered. "You'll be billed for the balance." He looked at me for a reaction.

Dad spoke quickly. "The money isn't a problem. We'll work that out."

Dr. Tesi seemed satisfied. "Another problem," he said, "is the cost of medication afterward. At first it can be a thousand dollars a month. The dosage will go down a little over the years, but you'll have to take anti-rejection medicines for the rest of your life. You can't miss a single day. Medicare doesn't cover these drugs. In-state patients usually qualify for some help from Ohio Medicaid, but that won't be an option for you."

I couldn't imagine coming up with an extra thousand dollars every month. I didn't respond, hoping Dr. Tesi would allow me to digest this later. He moved on.

"How quickly do you think you could get here from Georgia on short notice?"

"I guess I don't know. If I'm at home...if I'm packed and ready to go...if it isn't the middle of the night when planes aren't flying..."

I heard my own words. Too many *ifs*. I began to doubt this could be done. I closed my mouth and waited for the doctor to agree with my thoughts.

But he smiled and said, "You'll have about six hours. I think it can be done. You do have to stay close to home and check phone messages often. And make sure you're all the way ready to go when we call. Write a checklist for last-minute things. You should also know that you may have to make the trip more than once. Occasionally we find a donor, and by the time the patient reaches the hospital, something unpredictable happens. You could be sent back home to wait for another donor."

Dr. Tesi smiled reassuringly. "Don't worry. These are routine concerns, not likely to happen. I just want you to know how stressful the wait can be. And we never know how long it will take."

I finally relaxed, not because any of what lay ahead sounded easy, but because suddenly it seemed this might really happen. Barring any unusual test results, I would likely be placed on OSU's waiting list. Everything else would work out somehow.

I produced a notebook from my bag. Dr. Tesi patiently answered the questions I had scribbled in it the night before, even though my chart was closed now, and my forty-five minute tape had run out.

"No, the surgery isn't especially risky. Less than one percent chance you'll die on the table."

"Yes, you'll have to stay near the hospital during your recovery."

"No, a family member can't donate a pancreas. They wouldn't live long without one. A cadaver donor will provide both kidney and pancreas."

"Yes, you'll keep your existing organs. Your kidneys will catch on that a new one has taken over, and they'll gradually wither. The pancreas isn't that smart. It will continue to do what it has always done. The new one will do all of that and then some—it will produce insulin."

I liked Dr. Tesi. I found his sense of humor unusual for a surgeon. He became serious again and asked about my vision loss. I told him how it had felt to become legally blind overnight when I was only twenty-four, how I had thought I would never again contribute anything worthwhile to anyone.

"I hope you don't still feel that way," he said. "You seem to be doing very well." He leafed through his notes. "I see you were a patient here at the time. Dr. Davidorff did some surgery?"

"That's right. He was wonderful. Unfortunately, I didn't see him first. Someone else did my laser treatments, and not very well. Dr. Davidorff did surgery to minimize the damage, but surgery beyond that seemed too risky."

"I'm sorry," Dr. Tesi said, and we moved on.

He asked then about my diabetes management. How much insulin, how often? Had it bothered me to take injections? Had I had trouble maintaining good blood sugar control?

I told him I had always been considered a brittle diabetic. Wide swings in blood sugar occurred with little variation in my diet and exercise. Setting the *brittle* excuse aside, I admitted I had not always been diligent about my diet. "I've done a lot better, now that I use a monitor at home," I explained, "but I've only had one for about five years."

"You won't have to do that any more," Dr. Tesi interrupted.

"Do what?"

"Test your blood sugar. Take insulin injections."

I couldn't imagine it.

"So what's next?" I asked when it seemed we had covered it all.

"You'll have some blood drawn back at home. Your doctor will get instructions for packaging and shipping samples to us. We'll start the matching process and request samples periodically during your wait. We'll call you as soon as you're officially on the list."

I wanted to know how long that might take, and how long after that to find a donor, but I couldn't bring myself to ask. So far, this had been so much easier than I had expected. I didn't want to seem impatient and greedy. It was out of my hands now.

As we all stood to leave, Dr. Tesi put an arm around my shoulder and smiled. "You know, we don't do a pancreas transplant just so you can eat Hershey bars."

Dad and I laughed.

"We're doing it to help preserve the vision you still have, and to protect your new kidney from future damage by diabetes. You'll have some new challenges, but you'll know what *normal* feels like."

Normal would be nice. Freedom from insulin injections and finger-sticking would be too good to be true. And although I had not been a complete stranger to Hershey bars, a *guilt-free* Hershey bar would be heaven.

20

By mid-January, I had been on the transplant waiting list for less than three months, a relatively short time. But every day had seemed like an eternity, our entire routine revolving around a single phone call, a call I anxiously awaited, prepared for, and dreaded, all at the same time.

I wasn't worrying about the surgery itself. From the day I learned that a kidney and pancreas transplant was possible, I assumed that when it happened—when, not if—it would all go smoothly. It was all those details that had me on edge, those dozens of things out of my control that had to come together before donor and recipient could.

Only a few details were entirely my responsibility. I had to avoid contagious sick people, and I had to stay near our home phone, checking messages whenever I returned from a brief outing. Cell phones weren't riding on every hip yet in 1991, so the phone requirement was difficult and kept me close to home all winter. Avoiding germs was easier since I was hibernating anyway.

On Saturday, January 12, when the sun appeared bright and beautiful through the living room window for the first time in a week, it seemed like an invitation to go out for a few errands. There had been so little to do around the house lately. During those few weeks after Christmas, I had obsessed about the laundry and dishes, the vacuuming and dusting, the trash, houseplants and checkbook—any kind of busywork to keep me from losing my mind. I had sorted every sock and Pledged every tabletop. The shorter my to-do list got, the longer the days seemed. Might as well go.

I gathered purse and keys, put on jacket and gloves, looked at my watch and counted. Ten minutes to Kroger, ten minutes there, ten minutes home. The phone rang just as I opened the door between house and garage. I ran back through the kitchen to the living room and picked up on the fourth ring—a close tie with the answering machine. *You have reached...*

I caught my breath and managed a *hello.*

I heard a woman's voice. "Carol? I'm calling to tell you it's likely we have a donor for you."

I couldn't speak.

She continued, "You should make arrangements to take the next available flight. Pack your bags, but don't leave for the airport until you hear from us again."

I assembled enough words to assure her I understood what she was asking me to do. *Uh-huh. Okay. I'll do that.* I hung up the phone with a clear plan in mind. A minute later I couldn't remember step one.

I knew from earlier conversations with the OSU staff that I would need to be at the hospital in Columbus within six hours of the second call. It was twelve noon. If a seat were available on a commercial flight that afternoon, I would meet the deadline. The six-seat private plane we had arranged as back-up at our local airport would probably not be needed. That was good news, as we had prearranged everything for that flight except how to pay for it.

I paced from room to room, changing my mind every few seconds about what to do first. I looked on a closet shelf for the suitcase already lying open on the guest room bed. My heart was pounding and my feet were moving, but I was getting nowhere.

I called Mick at work to let him know about the phone call. Trying to sound casual, I told him I'd call him again when I heard something more definite.

"Oh my gosh," he said. "Are you okay?"

"I'm fine," I lied, "but we shouldn't stay on the phone now."

Paralyzed by the enormity of what lay ahead, I tried to remember where my list was. It should have been on the coffee table, but it wasn't. It could have landed on the kitchen counter, but it hadn't.

I called Mick again. "I think you should come home. I can't seem to get it together."

"I was just heading for the door," he said. "I just need to let Steve know I'm leaving."

I called my parents, who were planning to pick us up at the Columbus airport. When Dad answered, I was brief. I told him they should be ready for my next call. "It's likely we'll be coming tonight."

Dad relayed the news to my mother, and I heard her say, "Oh no." I imagined her springing into action, preparing for every possibility. She would have rehearsed for this too. Thinking of her getting ready 600 miles away gave me the momentum I needed. She wouldn't fall apart at this moment, and I couldn't afford to either.

I wondered if I should eat something, if there was anyone else I should call, if there was a way to stop the mail on a Saturday. There I was again, focusing on everything but the task at hand.

Mick reached home in record time, looking as disconnected as I felt. Unsure of what needed to be done first—he couldn't be still, but he couldn't pack anything either—he went to the garage and lifted his bicycle down from its hooks. After a vigorous ten-minute ride around the neighborhood, he was back, calmer now and ready to help.

By then, I had reserved two seats on a late afternoon Delta flight. Now we were just waiting for the phone call that would steer us toward the Atlanta airport. The call came within the hour, and we were finally able to think clearly enough to finish packing, alert our neighbor that we were leaving, and drive to the airport.

The plane ride was only an hour and ten minutes. Both lost in our own thoughts, we leafed through Skymall Magazine without reading and sipped soft drinks and ate pretzels without tasting.

My parents were waiting when we reached the gate in Columbus. After a flurry of hugs and overlapping chatter, Dad went ahead to bring the car around while Mom, Mick, and I made our way through baggage claim to the curb outside.

"Dennis says 670 West is a straight shot now all the way from here to High Street," I announced as we piled our luggage and ourselves into the car.

"I think it is," Dad said, "but I don't think today's the day to try it."

I glanced at my watch every few minutes as we drove up the east and across the north sides of the outerbelt and down Highway 315 toward the hospital. I tried to be calm.

We reached the emergency room entrance right at dark. We stepped carefully across the parking lot, avoiding jagged patches of ice still lingering after last week's freezing temperatures. The area was eerily quiet for a Saturday night—no ambulances, no sirens, no one at the desk inside. We hovered close to the counter. I peered over its edge, where a full cup of coffee assured me someone would soon return.

"Oh, sorry," a young man said as he pushed through swinging doors. "I'm the only one here right now. Sign in please?" He produced a clipboard, its pen dangling from a string.

Mick took the clipboard and signed my name between lines too narrow for me to navigate. He looked at his watch and wrote the time—6:50.

The young man took the list from Mick and studied my name.

"The transplant department said we should check in here first," I said, wondering if I had heard this instruction correctly.

He picked up the phone and dialed. "Carol Wilson has signed in for the transplant department. Send her to admissions?"

He hung up and said, "Might as well wait here. The admissions office will be available in about ten minutes."

I pictured this initial call setting people in motion elsewhere in the hospital, but the pace seemed absurdly relaxed at this first desk. With nowhere to sit, we stood with my luggage and watched the clock on the wall. We had made our deadline, and now the schedule was in someone else's hands. Still, I worried that someone, somewhere, was dropping the ball.

When Pat arrived a few minutes later, I was immediately calm again. I hadn't known he was coming, but I should have expected it. "Nancy's on her way too," he said as he hugged me. "I called her just before I left work."

He greeted Mick. "How are you holding up?"

"Fine," Mick laughed. "*I'm* not having surgery."

Pat hugged my mother and asked Dad, "Okay to leave our cars in this lot?"

"I don't know why not. No one has told us otherwise." Dad looked out through the heavy glass doors. "There's Nancy now. She's got a headlight out."

Pat stood watching the parking lot, looking, he said, for the person or vehicle that might be carrying the organs designated for me.

"That's ridiculous," I told him. "You have no idea where they are."

We all shared his curiosity, though, as we hadn't been told anything about the method for transporting organs.

Pat spotted an orderly approaching the door with a Styrofoam to-go container. He pointed and said, "I'll bet they're in there."

We all laughed at his bad joke, and I realized how much tension there had been in the room. We laughed too loudly and too long, exhausted beyond good sense. The man at the desk finally instructed us to report to the admissions office.

The six of us crowded into the tiny office. A clerk pushed one paper after another across the desk for me to sign, making a tidy stack in front of her as I slid each one back. She attached a plastic name band to my wrist and directed us to the seventh floor. As we waited for the elevator, Natalie caught up with us, and then our group numbered seven. She had left work when she heard my news and driven to Columbus from her home in southeast Ohio.

When we reached my room, I sat down on the edge of the bed. Mick sat in a nearby chair while my family wandered off to find restrooms, telephones, and coffee. It was nearly 9:00, and the long day was beginning to catch up with me.

"Do you think I should spend the night?" Mick asked.

I was torn. I wanted some time alone just to breathe, but I didn't want to lie awake all night alone. Sleep seemed unlikely.

A no-nonsense nurse resolved my dilemma. "Mr. Wilson, you should go now and get some sleep. Carol will be very busy for the next few hours. Surgery is at six A.M., and tomorrow will be a long day for all of you."

My family appeared in my doorway then, one by one, to say goodnight and wish me well. All would go to my parents' house for a short night's sleep.

Mick put my jacket and suitcases in the closet and returned to my bedside. "Will you be able to sleep?"

"I don't know, but I'm sure I'll catch up tomorrow."

"I guess you will," he said. "I'll see you in the morning before they take you down to surgery."

He hugged me tightly, and then he was gone.

I had about a minute of breathe time before the procedures began. For the next two hours, doctors, nurses and technicians stepped around each other like well-trained soldiers, drawing blood, inserting tubes, checking my blood pressure and pulse, disinfecting my abdomen with Betadine, and serving me a chalky white laxative drink to insure I'd be empty by morning.

The activity in my room eventually slowed. The lights were dimmed, the hallway grew quiet, and I felt surprisingly relaxed. If I fall asleep, I thought, that will mark the point of no return. I closed my eyes anyway and slept soundly.

Mick and my parents were back at the hospital before dawn. All of my brothers and sisters arrived at different times over the next hour or two.

Only Mick was allowed into my room while I waited to be wheeled away. He sat down quietly on the edge of my bed and asked, "Are you afraid?"

He hugged me then, and for the first time, the tears came. I hadn't allowed myself to be afraid, but now he was giving me permission to stop pretending, to give in, to lose control. Until that moment, I had concentrated only on being strong and positive so my transplant could not fail. I had thought about how I would get through this, how I would feel afterward, how I would enjoy the rest of my life. I, I, I.

And then, like an arrow through the heart, someone else entered the picture, a family I didn't know yet, sitting somewhere grieving for the one they had lost. I was here, on the most amazing threshold of my life, because someone had died. My anonymous donor had at that moment become a real person. There was no time at all to think about it, but the weight of this realization hovered over me as my surgery drew near.

An orderly came and wheeled me briskly down the hall. Mick hurried alongside until he was allowed to go no further. Soon I was in a pristine white cubicle outside the operating room.

An anesthesiologist was preparing the solution that would ease me to sleep. Halfway through the procedure, a nurse arrived and quietly announced that a necessary match had not yet been made in the blood bank. It was unlikely I'd need a transfusion, but compatible blood had to be on hand just in case. The doctor saw the look on my face and said, "Minor glitch. Don't worry. I'll be right back." He set down his tools and left the room.

I wished I had been completely under before this oversight was discovered, oblivious to the delay. Instead, I lay there too wide awake and too aware of time. Here I am, I thought, five minutes from rescue and drowning in someone else's mistake.

I pictured myself wheeled up a moment too late to the operating room door and watching it close like a missed elevator. I didn't know what a kidney or pancreas would look like on the other side of that door, lying in wait to be reconnected in a stranger's body. I knew they didn't beat like a heart, but I imagined them giving up, unable to wait, while I lay a few feet away coming undone.

I looked around me, though, and no one else seemed alarmed. *Shouldn't these people be tripping all over each other to get this problem solved?* I finally resigned myself to the truth. From this point on, I was not in charge of *anything.* I managed not to speak. Time to trust.

The anesthesiologist returned and resumed his work, hooking me up to a slow-dripping IV. I was getting drowsy already as I entered the operating room. I couldn't tell doctors from nurses in their green scrubs, white masks, and paper-covered shoes. They moved quickly and efficiently, in remarkably good humor for such an early hour. I protested when an attendant arranged me in an awkward position on the table.

He responded with a grin. "That's nothing. We'll have you twisted up like a pretzel before it's all over."

I was so relaxed, my laugh didn't sound like my own. A voice asked if I was getting sleepy.

"Uh-huh."

"Start counting backward now from a hundred," another voice said.

"Okay. Do a good job. One hundred, ninety-nine..."

For the next six hours, my family camped out in a large atrium near the operating room. They visited, napped, read, knitted, played solitaire, drank coffee, gambled, prayed, and impatiently watched the door, eager for a report from within.

The report came directly from my surgeon, Dr. Ferguson. The news was good. "She's doing well. The transplant went perfectly."

21

By late afternoon, I was beginning to emerge from the anesthesia. An aide checked my vital signs, a nurse encouraged me to sit up and cough, and a doctor and his students discussed my surgery.

I wanted to see my husband and my family, but what I focused on were bits of conversation among the staff. I hoped they weren't asking me questions—I felt unable to respond—but I strained to hear what they were saying about my surgery.

The kidney is working well and the bladder is emptying efficiently.

Blood sugar is normal and stable, with no insulin injections since noon yesterday.

Then from somewhere amid the white uniforms, I heard a voice: *It was a ten-year-old girl.*

And then I was drifting again.

I became aware that a hand was offering me a shiny ice chip on a pink plastic spoon. It was Mick. He had talked his way past three nurses to gain early entry to the recovery room. He told me later that he was shocked at how I looked those first few hours and understood then why he had been encouraged to wait a while. He couldn't see my entire body, but my face was as round and orange as a pumpkin. I had been painted all over with an iodine solution, and fourteen pints of fluid had been dripped into my veins during surgery.

"The excess fluid will encourage and require the new kidney to begin its work," a nurse explained to Mick.

"She keeps saying it hurts," he told her. "Can you do something?"

"It's just the incision. The transplanted organs have no nerves, so they can't register pain. She's getting medication. And don't worry, she won't remember this pain."

The nurse was right. By the end of the next day—in my own room now and hooked up to fewer gadgets—I felt wonderful. I couldn't imagine staying a whole week.

The first several days were so busy, the time went quickly. I had visitors all day, every day, most of them bearing edible gifts. My diet was unrestricted now, and word spread quickly.

Dr. Tesi, the doctor who had interviewed me back in October, called on me often, always leading a group of students, lecturing casually as they walked. They studied the dry-erase chart on the wall next to my bed, where my lab results were posted throughout the day.

I encouraged everyone to help themselves to my array of goodies—a one-pound Hershey's Kiss, a package of Oreos, a bag of trail mix, Hostess cupcakes—and there was still more than my bedside table would hold. Students seemed unsure whether they should "eat in class," but Dr. Tesi ate freely from my stash, often leaving my room with a mouthful of something and a handful of something else. I suspected he came in sometimes just to see what was new at my snack bar.

I enjoyed the treats, but for the first time in twenty-seven years, I didn't crave them. I ate what I wanted, when I wanted, but one treat no longer led to a desire for another. Best of all, I didn't wonder with every bite what the damage would be.

After several days, when I had sampled all the previously forbidden foods put before me, I became cautious about my eating. My primary nurse, Mary Jane, warned me, "The Prednisone you'll be taking for the rest of your life will make you very hungry. Put a padlock on your refrigerator, or you'll have a real problem with weight gain."

Mary Jane quickly became my favorite nurse. She was assigned to my case most days, but she spent more time with me than was required. Acknowledging my visual limitations, she read to me printed information that would otherwise have been a struggle with my magnifier. She marked the tops of my many medicine bottles with a thick magic marker so I wouldn't mistake one for another.

I had brought with me some cotton yarn and knitting needles and set about crafting simple dish cloths. I had learned to knit as a young child and could still do an easy knit-purl without actually seeing the stitches. At the end of each evening, when Mary Jane's shift had ended, she sat for a few minutes and examined my project, rescuing any stitches I had lost during the day. Sometimes the repairs looked a little odd, having been made many rows after the fact, but the cloths held together, thanks to her patience.

My family liked Mary Jane too. They had all met her while I was still in recovery. One day, when she was explaining to me about the Cyclosporine I would be taking to suppress my immunity and prevent rejection, she gave me a pamphlet about its side effects. Some were troubling: hormonal changes, inability to fight infection, susceptibility to cancer.

"Read this sometime," she said, "but maybe don't show your dad." She confided that she had already pegged Mick as the impatient one and Dad as the worrier.

On Tuesday evening, two days after surgery, I was feeling so well, I encouraged Mick to return home. I knew he was getting bored between hospital visits. I also hoped he would have vacation days left when I returned to Georgia in a month.

"Are you sure?" he asked as I wrote the Delta Airlines number on a scrap of paper.

I handed it to him. "I'm sure. You could stay another day or another week, and my routine would be the same. You'll enjoy being home."

Mick flew back to Atlanta the next morning, took one more day off to get the house in order, and returned to work on Friday.

The pace slowed a little after that. My parents, not yet fully retired, returned to their jobs. They visited some evenings, as did my siblings, nieces and nephews, but my days were quiet.

A representative from LOOP, Lifeline of Ohio Organ Procurement, came to my room one afternoon and explained to me that I could, if I chose to, write an anonymous letter to my donor's family. Of course this sounded like something I wanted to do. I responded enthusiastically to her suggestion.

"Don't be concerned," the woman advised, "if you don't get a response. Some families choose not to receive these letters."

Surprised by this, I asked, "How will I know whether to send one then?"

"Oh," she said, handing me an envelope preprinted with LOOP's address, "you can give or send your letter to us. Our records will show whether the family chose to accept letters. If they did, we'll send yours on."

I vowed to write my letter first thing in the morning. What in the world would I say to this family? I didn't even know their name, and I knew nothing of the circumstances surrounding their daughter's death. I thought about it for the rest of the evening. How to begin? Dear Donor Family? Dear Friend? Was I even sure enough about what I had overheard to mention *how sorry I am about your daughter*? When just the greeting kept me awake into the night, I knew this would not be as easy as it had sounded.

My crumpled third draft had just missed the waste basket when Mary Jane breezed in the next morning. She scooped up the ball of paper and held it up between thumb and forefinger. "What's up?"

Trying not to sound frustrated, because it seemed I should be so filled with gratitude the words would pour out onto the page, I said, "I can't get this letter to my donor's family to come out right."

She gave me a sympathetic smile. "There is no *right*. It can be two words or two lines or two pages. And there's no time limit. You can write it now or you can wait until you've come to terms with it all." She leaned over and gave me a quick hug.

"Thank you," I said. "For everything."

I asked Mary Jane if she had some nicer paper. My spiral notebook pages with their holes and ragged edges didn't seem appropriate. She brought me an ample stack of copy machine paper. I set it aside. Just for a few days, I thought, and then I'll try again.

The following Thursday, twelve days after surgery, I was discharged from the hospital and went to my parents' house just north of Columbus to continue my recovery.

"This will be a critical time," Dr. Tesi explained. "You'll need to stay here in the area so we can monitor your blood-work and watch for signs of rejection. At least three more weeks. We'll find a lab for you near your folks so you won't have to come here every other day."

I hadn't allowed myself to dwell on the possibility of rejection, but doctors and nurses had advised me that many transplant patients experience a rejection episode, usually reversible if caught in time, within the first several weeks.

"After that," Dr. Tesi said, "the risk decreases somewhat, and you'll need labwork less often."

It was an easy, comfortable time at Mom and Dad's, with visits from family, dinner out with friends Mick and I were still close to in Columbus, an evening at my nephew's junior high basketball game, and some quiet afternoons with my sister Nancy, still feeling adrift after losing her husband. Mom and Dad coordinated their schedules so one of them could get me to the lab and back early in the morning every Monday, Wednesday, and Friday.

After about a week, the days began to seem long. I had too much energy to be sitting around so much. Mom left no chores undone, so I could find little to help out with around the house. I missed my husband and my cat, my household routine and my golf cart. I missed winter in the South, where we could step outside for a few minutes without coat, hat and gloves.

I was ready to get back to my life, to dive into all the projects I had set aside while waiting for my transplant. I made long, detailed lists of the loose ends I would tie up as soon as I could get back to Georgia.

Three weeks after surgery, I was due for a follow-up visit at the hospital. I was elated to see Dr. Tesi enter the examining room. Of all the doctors who had cared for me during my hospital stay, he had become my favorite. Now he was assigned to my post-transplant care.

My incision had flattened to a tidy pink seam, about five inches long from my navel straight down. Dr. Tesi pressed the bulge just to the left, the location of my new kidney, and then did the same on the right, my pancreas. I felt no discomfort at all.

I commented on the length of the scar and said I guessed my bikini days were over.

"Couldn't put 'em in with a straw," he said, referring to my new organs. He pronounced me in good working order, and the exam was over.

We talked as we went down the hall toward the elevator. I asked him where he was going for his afternoon snacks, now that I was gone. He said, "I really thought your family would just keep bringing them."

We waited for a slower than usual elevator while he gave me last-minute instructions to continue my labwork, to report any fever or pain, to drink at least three quarts of water per day, and to take it easy at my mom's for another week.

"Dr. Tesi," I interrupted, "I'd like to go home."

The elevator door opened, and I watched it close without getting on. He gave me a puzzled look. "Oh, you can. We're finished for today."

I spoke carefully then, realizing this was a long shot. "I mean, home to Georgia."

He crossed his arms and looked at me. "You promised you'd stay in town for a month."

I should have given up then, should have let him off the hook. I had promised the four weeks without question when he and his staff had agreed to accept me, an out-of-state patient, into their transplant program. It had seemed a reasonable request, an easy promise to make.

But I tried again. "I'm sure my husband is about ready for a romantic evening. I'd like to be there for that."

He laughed and shook his head. I could see he was giving in. Without further discussion, we wandered away from the elevator and settled into two vacant chairs in the hallway. He located a discharge form in his stack of papers and started to write. I was going home.

My instructions were a little different now. I'd have my blood drawn at an Atlanta hospital three times a week, and results would be faxed to Dr. Tesi for his review. His final warning was, "If we call and tell you you've got a problem, you'll need to drop everything and head for the airport. You'll have to get right back here. Will you do that?"

Another easy promise to make, not negotiable this time.

Hugs were longer than usual the next day as my parents stood with me at the departure gate. They seemed reluctant to have me going home ahead of schedule, but I knew they were ready too, to have their lives back. They would go to bed early or sleep in late, skip breakfast if they wanted. With fewer visitors, Mom would have less winter slush tramped into her kitchen, and Dad would have his upstairs bathroom to himself again. The dog would reclaim her couch space, and the house would be quiet again.

I wanted to spend my flight time gathering my thoughts, processing all that had happened to me in three short weeks, imagining being back home.

The man next to me started a conversation as soon as I buckled myself in. "Is Columbus home for you, or is Atlanta?"

I told him, "All of my family are here in Ohio, but my husband and I moved from here about twelve years ago, first to North Carolina and then to the Atlanta area."

"Just came for a visit then?" he continued.

"A visit and a transplant," I said, without considering this might create a longer conversation than either of us wanted. So much for my hour of quiet reflection.

When we were airborne, he wanted to know all the details: Why did I need a transplant, how long was I on the waiting list, was the surgery risky, was it successful?

And then, "Was someone in your family a match?"

"Well, they were," I said, "but it couldn't be done that way. A kidney can be donated by a living person, but a pancreas can't. I needed both, and both had to come from the same cadaver."

I hated the word *cadaver*. It was a way to avoid *person*, *girl*, and *child*. "My donor was a ten-year-old girl," I said, surprised by my own words. I couldn't remember having said them before.

For almost an hour, I talked to a stranger on a plane about something I hadn't found a way to talk to anyone else about. I didn't know if any of it mattered to him, but I couldn't end it there. I hadn't realized I needed to tell someone, but the telling felt good.

I was feeling tired by the time we landed, maybe from the roller coaster I had been on since leaving home for Ohio, or maybe from pouring my story onto this man's lap. He had handled it well, his curiosity changing quickly to genuine interest, and with such sadness and empathy for my donor's family, I felt guilty about having given them so little thought. He wished me "the best of luck" as we stood to reach our carry-ons.

Mick was waiting at the end of the jetway, so close to the door frame my shoulder brushed against him before I recognized him. We held each other and held up the line as impatient passengers worked their way around us. Atlanta's Hartsfield International was, as usual, noisy and congested. We started down the concourse toward the escalator leading to the underground train. I rolled my suitcase along and tried to keep up as Mick carved a path for me through the crowd.

Settled in the car and paid up at the parking booth, we were finally able to catch our breath and have a real conversation. We were able to, but we didn't.

"Chinese?" Mick asked.

"Oh, that sounds *really good*," I said, glad to be relieved of more heavy discussion. It was four o'clock already, and I hadn't eaten all day. I hadn't even thought about food.

Dragon Lady, a restaurant Mick had discovered while I was away, was just a few blocks from home. We stopped there for an early dinner. Mick had obviously become a familiar face there. An overly attentive waiter hovered as we ate, so we still had little opportunity to talk about anything beyond flight conditions and won ton soup. We both needed a return to a normal routine, and we enjoyed just having dinner together again.

When we got home, I admired the house, pleased that it was clean and tidy—no dishes in the sink and no clothes on the floor. The bathroom needed some Comet, but that could wait.

Mick appeared in the bathroom doorway. "Looking for something?"

"No," I said, opening and closing the medicine cabinet door. I had just noticed how empty the counter was. Much of its surface had stored my insulin, syringes, alcohol swabs, and testing supplies. Mick had tucked them away somewhere. Had he been optimistic enough to throw them away?

I realized then what it was going to be like not to wake up and face all of that every morning. The absence of diabetic gear hadn't had much impact in the hospital—there had been enough needles and lab tests to take its place—but here at home, this bare, white counter seemed like a clean slate for a new beginning.

22

I wanted to spend my first full day at home pampering my cat and driving my golf cart to the grocery store, filling the fridge with food, and cooking an elaborate dinner for Mick. But I had just one day to find a local lab and arrange for my blood to be drawn three days a week. After several phone calls, I found an independent lab who offered to send a technician to my house. I hadn't known such a service existed, but I was relieved that at least for a while, I wouldn't have to arrange early morning transportation to a hospital, the nearest of which was a half hour from Peachtree City.

The lab procedure went smoothly that first week. At 7:30 every other morning, while I was still padding around in robe and slippers and Mick was dressing for work, a bespectacled, middle-aged man arrived carrying a small tray of supplies. It looked like the lift-out tray from a tool box. It held test tubes with stoppers of various colors, a pair of white latex gloves, an elastic tourniquet, a syringe connected to a length of thin, clear tubing, and a folded piece of paper—lab orders from OSU, I guessed. The man was precise and efficient, in and out in less than ten minutes, and then the rest of the day was mine.

It was mid-February and still flu season, so on Friday, the end of my first week at home, when I developed a cough and slight fever, I thought maybe I had picked up a bug somewhere. I had stayed close to home, but it wasn't impossible I had been exposed on my flight home, at the pharmacy, or by the lab technician who had been making house calls. After he left that morning, I climbed back into bed and pulled up all the covers. My face felt hot, but I started to shiver in spite of two blankets and a comforter. I got up and took two Tylenol with two glasses of water, and by noon, my temperature had fallen from 101 to 99. My cough was persistent, though, and I couldn't take a deep breath without choking.

I didn't want to overreact to a simple cold or go and sit in my doctor's waiting room and expose myself to something worse. With the weekend approaching, I was also afraid to do nothing.

I decided to just take it easy for the rest of the day and load up on fluids. Feeling a little better after chicken noodle soup, orange juice and applesauce, I assumed I'd be fine by morning.

When Mick called at six to say he was leaving work and would be home shortly, my fever had returned. When he reached home, I sat bundled in blankets on the couch, shivering again, cold on the inside and hot on the outside.

We debated whether we should go to the emergency room, but decided to give it a few more hours. "Tylenol is helping," I assured him, "and drinking water."

"We should probably go," Mick urged. "Emergency rooms get crazy late at night."

"If I'm not feeling any better by nine, I'll go," I finally agreed, "but I think it's just the flu."

Our indecision ended when the phone rang an hour later. I stood at the kitchen wall phone and heard a familiar voice on the line. It was a transplant coordinator I had spoken with several times prior to my surgery.

"Dr. Tesi just reviewed your lab numbers from this morning. They don't look very good. Your potassium is dangerously high, and your carbon dioxide is low. Are you feeling okay?"

"Not really," I admitted, "but I think I just caught a bug. I'm actually feeling better tonight than I have all day."

I couldn't make myself ask the question that had nagged at me all afternoon. *Am I having a rejection?*

She answered it anyway with her instructions. "Have your labs repeated first thing in the morning and have results faxed as soon as they're available. We'll go from there. Pack a bag in case we need you back here tomorrow."

I had questions, but I knew she was only the messenger. I swallowed hard and thanked her for calling.

"Not good?" Mick asked as I hung up the phone.

"Not good. I have to find a place to have blood drawn early in the morning. Ohio will look at the results and call me. I might have to go back. Something's wrong."

I wandered into the bedroom and halfheartedly packed an overnight bag. The small effort required to gather toothbrush and toothpaste, deodorant, and a few nightclothes left me fatigued and out of breath. I was feeling warm again, and cold, and my heart was racing. Sitting down slowed my heart rate and made breathing easier, so I told Mick I thought I should go to bed early.

"I'll go too," he said. "Tomorrow could be a long day."

I went to bed hoping against hope that I had packed a bag for nothing, but I knew better. I drifted off to sleep feeling as defeated as I had ever felt. I wondered if a child's organs had been unable to survive the demands of my adult body. I felt guilty that they might have had a better chance in a body undamaged by diabetes.

Mick and I drove to a hospital on Atlanta's far north side early Saturday morning. Their emergency room doctor had agreed by phone to allow me to have blood drawn there as an outpatient. The nurse who checked me in asked for the name of my local referring physician. I provided the first name that came to mind, Dr. Fulton, the Atlanta doctor who had first diagnosed my kidney failure five months earlier.

"My orders are from Ohio State University, though," I explained. "That's where results should go, as soon as you get them."

We were back home by eleven. Mick wondered if he should go on to work and finish out the day. I encouraged him to do that.

"What if they call and say you need to come?" he asked.

"I'll go by myself this time."

He smiled sadly, but I thought he seemed relieved. I couldn't have described what I was feeling, except that I needed to be alone.

I boarded the plane back to Ohio late that afternoon, flying solo this time and not sharing the reason for my trip with any strangers. My lab results had come back the same as the day before. I didn't know what would happen when I reached the hospital. I hadn't wanted to ask that question.

My arrival in Columbus was similar to the time before, my parents retrieving me at the Delta gate and driving me to the hospital. Our stop at the admissions office was brief this time, and then I settled into a double room on the seventh floor. Some of the staff were familiar to me, but the mood so late on a Saturday night was all business.

I awoke after a restless night to the sound of Dr. Tesi's voice.

"You're back," he said when I looked up at him. "I'm not surprised."

I was offended at first, but then he explained, "This kind of rejection episode usually happens right at a month. Don't worry. We expect it, and we can usually fix it."

I had avoided the word *rejection*. Even the thought of it had stirred a flutter of panic in my stomach throughout the night. But my doctor's calm voice assured me that all was not necessarily lost.

"You're severely dehydrated," he continued. "An IV will resolve that. Then you'll drink a delicious concoction that will flush out your excess potassium. It's at a critical level."

I asked him if dehydration could cause rejection.

He shrugged. "It can aggravate a rejection already in progress."

A rejection in progress. I couldn't believe this was really happening. When Dr. Tesi had gone, I turned on my side, away from the door, and buried my head in my pillow. The girl sharing my room was struggling with serious complications of her own. I didn't want her to hear me cry.

As I tried to fall back to sleep, I felt a tug on my covers.

"I'm not on this floor today, but I saw your name on the admissions list. What's up?"

It was Mary Jane.

"I don't know what's up," I said, the tears beginning again. "This is the first time I ever thought this might not work."

She sat on the edge of the bed and put her arms around me. "It is going to work. You'll have a kidney biopsy later today. If it shows you're having a rejection, they'll treat you right away." She looked at her watch and stood to go. "I'll check on you again before I leave tonight."

The biopsy late that afternoon confirmed I was having a rejection episode. A doctor numbed my abdomen, inserted a large needle through my skin into the new kidney, and extracted a thin plug of tissue for testing.

"The tissue shows changes consistent with rejection," Dr. Tesi explained when he arrived the next morning. "We'll watch your labs for the rest of the day, then probably start treatment at bedtime."

The day seemed endless. I wondered what this treatment would be like and why it wouldn't begin until nighttime.

Nancy arrived at six and stayed beyond the end of visiting hours. I started to understand what my night would be like when a nurse told her, "You'll want to go now. It's going to be a very long night."

Nancy didn't get up from her chair. She made no move at all toward leaving. I could see she was afraid for me.

"You should go," I said, "before the parking garage gets dark and deserted."

She reluctantly gathered her jacket and purse and eased toward the door. "Are you sure?"

"I'll be fine," I said. "See you tomorrow."

When Nancy had gone, a doctor and three residents gathered at my bedside. They discussed the medicine I would receive. The doctor described it as "a nasty drug called Minnesota Orthoklone T-III, or OKT-3 for short." He asked his students, "Who's here overnight? Galbo?"

A dark-haired, olive-skinned young man looked down at the floor and slowly raised his hand. Dr. Galbo's reluctance to acknowledge his assignment should have been a clue. But I had tolerated nasty drugs before, and I had endured enough medical procedures to know they all had a beginning and an end, a predictable amount of discomfort for a predictable length of time.

"Eight hours," Dr. Galbo announced when he returned by himself a half hour later, pushing a cartful of supplies. "You're going to have a miserable eight hours. I'm sorry."

Two nurses stood by while he prepared me for the procedure. "OKT-3 is a powerful new antirejection medicine. I'm going to inject it slowly into your IV. You'll have a flu-like reaction for the next several hours. It's going to be a long night." He smiled then and added, "You will *hate* mice by morning."

I laughed. "Mice?"

"The serum," he said. "It comes from mice."

He counted under his breath, a precise sixty seconds, as he eased a small syringeful of OKT-3 into my IV. Then we waited, the nurses still hovering, for the drug to make its way through my body.

I didn't know what they had been trained to watch for. I expected the flu symptoms I had experienced only a few times in my life—headache, fever, an achy body. When Dr. Galbo stood to leave and instructed the nurses, "I'm here all night. Call me if her temperature reaches 105," I braced myself for the worst.

My temperature rose over the next few hours. The nurses took turns checking my vital signs, cooling my forehead with wet cloths, and removing layers of bedding one by one as I tossed and turned. I heard them report to each other each time the thermometer climbed another degree. At 103, my muscles began to cramp. I clenched my fists and pressed my knees together tightly to keep them from shaking. I ground my teeth and pulled my knees up to my chest when the pain became more intense at 104.

The nurses brought more cold cloths, tucking them now under my arms, behind my knees, and under the small of my back. Moving for them was painful, but the fresh, wet cloths felt good while their coolness lasted.

For the next several hours, I shivered and sweated, twisted and stretched, trying to find a position that didn't hurt. I gripped my legs so tightly I caused bruises between my knees and on my wrists and forearms. Several times, I heard the nurses discuss whether they should call the doctor. If they did, and if he came, I didn't know it.

During the worst part of the night, the middle, I was barely aware of the activity around me. I concentrated on voices, determined not to lose consciousness. At my most delirious moment, I thought about asking a nurse if she would call my husband and my family, because I thought I might not survive.

During that terrible hour, I stared at the white circle I knew was a clock high on the wall opposite my bed. The numbers and hands weren't bold enough for me to see, but I imagined the second hand ticking away, and I counted. Eventually, I was able to relax my entire body for a few seconds at a time, and then for a few minutes.

When I finally saw a stream of daylight through the blinds across the room, the pounding in my head was beginning to ease. The nurses no longer stood by. I heard a new shift arriving in the hallway. I slept then, too exhausted to vacate my bed for a change of sheets and hospital gown.

When Mary Jane woke me a few hours later to give me my morning pills, I saw that my mother was there. She sat knitting a blue slipper, watching the television with the sound turned down.

"Rough night," she said when I looked her way.

An observation, not a question. My hair was matted, my gown twisted around my legs, my bedding in damp disarray.

"Rough isn't the word for it."

Still too weak to sit up on my own, I cranked up the head of my bed, and then pressed another button to give my knees a bend. By noon, I wanted food and something to drink, a shower, and clean, dry sheets. I slid to the edge of the bed, and Mom helped me to a nearby chair to make room for the aide with the linens. I still needed sleep, but I was beginning to feel almost normal again.

When Dr. Tesi told me that afternoon, "Your labwork is coming around nicely. I think we've turned the corner," I was relieved. My relief turned to dread when he added, "You'll have your second dose of OKT-3 tonight at bedtime, then every day for a total of ten."

I gave him a look that implied he had lost his mind. "Nine more days?"

Dr. Tesi quickly continued, "The first night is the worst. Tonight will be much easier."

"*Anything* would be easier than last night," I said.

He smiled apologetically. "It's working."

That was what I needed to hear, that it had been worth it. My brief thoughts of refusing another treatment disappeared.

After the injection of OKT-3 that night, I slept until morning with only a mild fever. After four more days, Dr. Tesi allowed me to continue treatment at my parents' house. A visiting nurse came each morning for four days to draw my blood and give me an injection of OKT-3 by IV. I felt lightheaded after these treatments, but the feeling lasted less than an hour.

At my follow-up exam on the Monday after my last treatment, where Dr. Tesi pronounced me "good as new," he allowed me to return home to Georgia. I had been caught so off guard by this rejection episode, I felt uneasy about going. I asked Dr. Tesi, "What should I watch for in my lab numbers so this doesn't happen again? I sure didn't know it this time."

An arm around my shoulder, he said kindly, "You're doing just fine. Keep doing what you're supposed to. Don't miss any medicine. Keep all your lab appointments, take your temperature and blood pressure every day, and call post-transplant if you have a fever over 101 that doesn't respond to Tylenol. You do the day-to-day, and we'll keep track of the nuts and bolts. And one more thing. Be sure to get the best medical care you can find down south."

We both laughed as he continued, "You're a Rolls Royce now, not a Ford. You can't let just anybody work on you."

23

I did feel like a Rolls Royce when I returned home that second time. My energy seemed endless, my mood ecstatic. It was a feeling of well-being I had enjoyed for only brief intervals during my years with diabetes. This was how normal was supposed to feel.

Although my doctors hadn't belabored the point, I was aware that some transplant patients suffer repeated rejection episodes or catastrophic transplant failures. But I felt confident that my rejection troubles were behind me. The memory of my OKT-3 ordeal faded quickly.

For the next five years, I enjoyed complete freedom from diabetes, freedom from even thinking about it. I had imagined that after so many years dependent on insulin, I might wake up every morning and reach for a syringe and a vial of insulin, or that I would feel a guilt pang whenever something sweet touched my tongue. Such thoughts never entered my mind. It was as though my years with diabetes had just been a long detour on my way to the life I was meant to have.

During those first five years after transplant, I tried to express this feeling in letters to my donor's family. I abandoned the effort each time, wondering if my words could ever express my gratitude for this new life. Each rough draft left me feeling it couldn't be done with paper and pen.

As the months and years went by, I tried less and less often. Eventually I decided so much time had passed, any letter, regardless of its message, would seem too little, too late. I allowed myself no more guilt about a letter I would never send.

One afternoon in the fall of 1996, I found our mailbox partly open with a thick manila envelope stuffed inside. The envelope curled around the inside of the box, sticking out the end like a sleeping bag that won't fit back into its canvas sleeve. I tugged it from the box and took it inside, laying it on the kitchen table while I went about my household routine. I had been expecting this package, but I didn't expect it would hold any surprises. I let it lie there for several days, moving it aside with all the other paper clutter whenever I needed table space.

A few weeks earlier, I had requested my medical records from Ohio State University because I had made an appointment to see a new internist, my own having taken a short leave of absence. I thought the new doctor should have access to more information than I could provide on the short lines of a medical history form. I'd just take the whole fat file with me to his office, and the record-keepers there could sort it all out.

After about a week, it occurred to me that some pages of that file would probably be repetitious or unimportant. Maybe I should trim it down before handing it over.

I sat down with a bright light and a magnifier and started to read. Most of the reports were purely technical, but I felt compelled to look at everything. Some of the pages described the new way my insides had been hooked up, with all the surgical detail, down to the actual length of the vessels connecting new kidney and new pancreas to original bladder. Some pages were all about the chemistry, others about the plumbing.

I read some each day, stopping whenever the words started to swim and the crick in my neck began to seem permanent. The pages were sometimes quite boring, but the sheer volume of information made me want to get through all of it. Unless I copied the entire file, several dozen pages, further access to my transplant story would be limited. So I continued to read.

About halfway through the stack, I found a piece of paper so different from the rest, it demanded my full attention. On the left side of the page was a column filled with numbers and letters called *markers*. Beyond blood type, markers show how closely the blood of an organ donor matches that of a recipient. This section didn't mean much to me at the time. I knew already that my donor and I had been an exceptionally close match. I moved then to the upper right side of the page. And there she was. My donor had a name.

Jami Snyder, Age 10, Female, Blood Type A

I was listed there too.

Carol Wilson, Age 37, Female, Blood Type A

I stared at her name for a long time, then crossed my arms on the page, put my head down, and cried. I wandered around the house the rest of the day, disconcerted and numb, grieving as though I had just learned this child had died.

Jami's age was not a surprise. I had learned that much about her on the day of my transplant. But now that she had a name, she also had a favorite color, a fifth grade teacher, a Christmas stocking, a best friend. Did she have a mischievous spirit? Trouble with math? Fear of the dark? And did I want to know?

What I wanted was either to erase her name from my mind, or to know everything about her. The first would prove impossible; the second was a choice I would make many years later.

24

For the next seven years, I was content knowing only Jami's name. Knowing it gave me a peaceful feeling about her and allowed me to stop thinking of her as a cadaver donor. Now I could speak her name and breathe a prayerful thank-you whenever my life took a turn for the better—when I received a good medical report, when an eye exam showed no deterioration in my vision, when Mick and I reached our twenty-fifth anniversary, when we celebrated my fiftieth birthday. *Thank you, Jami.*

I'm not sure what encouraged me to learn more about Jami in the summer of 2003. I just started wondering again what she was like.

I had never believed the claims people made that after a transplant, they took on characteristics of their donors—a sudden distaste for the ice cream flavor they had always loved or a new talent for drawing. But I did wish for Jami to have had a childhood similar to mine, happy and secure. She probably had kind parents like mine, I thought. Uncaring parents would not donate their child's organs. And she might have been a bit of a tomboy like me, not a frilly little girl. After all, her mother had named her Jami, not Tiffany or Alexandra. These were just guesses, though. I wanted to know more.

Not adept yet at internet navigation, I made a phone call to Ohio's Department of Health. The woman I spoke with treated my request as routine. "You can get copies of birth and death certificates by requesting them in writing and enclosing a check for two dollars."

It would be as easy as that if Jami lived and died in Ohio. Other states would require separate searches. Since less than twenty-four hours had elapsed between my call to report to the hospital in Ohio and my transplant surgery, I assumed my transplant organs had not had time to travel cross-country. I would begin with Ohio, even though I knew it was a long shot. Snyder was a fairly common name, and Jami might have been a nickname. She could have been born anywhere, could have died somewhere else.

I sent my request and assumed it would turn up nothing. I would give it up then, and never know.

A week later, I received a letter from the Department of Health telling me they were unable to provide the information I had asked for. I was disappointed, but I talked myself out of looking any further. *You aren't entitled to know about your donor. There is probably a good reason recipients aren't given easy access to this information.*

Two days later, I was surprised to find another envelope from the health department in the mailbox. I set it aside with the rest of the mail, assuming the envelope held my two dollar check. When I opened it later that evening, I saw two photocopied documents—a birth certificate and a death certificate—both in the name of Jami Mari Snyder.

I sat there at the kitchen table, thinking maybe I shouldn't read through the documents, but knowing I would. The documents were short, but I studied them into the night, putting together the pieces of Jami's history. I learned that she was born in a Springfield, Ohio hospital in the middle of the afternoon on April 14, 1980, attended by a nurse-midwife. Her father Douglas, twenty years old, born in Ohio, and her mother Jacqueline, twenty-four, born in Germany, lived on Cedar Street in Springfield.

I lingered over Jami's birth certificate, reading between the lines and drawing conclusions about her life, in order to delay moving on to her death. I calculated that she had been born on a Monday. Was that the day for children "full of grace?" Cedar Street brought to mind a neighborhood with trees and sidewalks, yards with clotheslines and swing sets. Springfield had a pleasant sound too. I located it in an old highway atlas, near Dayton, less than forty miles from my Columbus home. I wondered if Jami's mother was German and decided it was more likely Jami's maternal grandparents had been stationed overseas for a time in the military.

When I could find no more dots to connect, I turned apprehensively to the next page. I had never seen a death certificate before. Longer and more detailed than the birth certificate, it provided a jagged road map from birth to burial. Each time I encountered a space marked N/A, not applicable, I was reminded how short Jami's journey had been. She had not lived long enough to attend secondary school or college, to serve in the military, to marry, or to have an occupation.

This document, unlike the birth certificate, didn't cause my mind to wander quietly through Jami's childhood neighborhood. I couldn't soften the edges of this report.

Jami suffered *blunt impact injuries of the head*, received while a passenger in an automobile accident on Saturday, January 5, 1991.

I paused here, wondering about the date and realizing she must have survived a week with her injuries.

Jami died in Dayton's Children's Medical Center at 1:15 in the afternoon on Saturday, January 12.

After reading this, I was positive for the first time that Jami was my donor. The details I had overheard, stumbled upon, and pieced together over the past twelve years had left room for a small, but nagging doubt. The timing was undeniable now. Jami's death and my call to report to Ohio for surgery had occurred on the same day and within the same hour.

Although finding out about Jami through public records didn't seem inappropriate to me, doing so out of mere curiosity did feel like a breach of an unwritten code among transplant recipients, their donors, and their doctors. I needed to give purpose to my search, to make it right, at least within my own heart. I wanted more than ever to find a way to thank Jami's family.

Again I considered writing an anonymous letter and sending it through Lifeline of Ohio. I wondered if such a letter would reach the right person at the right address after so many years. On Jami's death certificate, her mother's last name was no longer Snyder. It appeared as Jacqueline Eichelberger, and her address had changed. Perhaps she had divorced and remarried. If she chose not to respond, I would always wonder if the letter had reached her.

I decided I would find a way to contact Jami's mother personally, even if only briefly and only once, to thank her and to assure her that Jami's gift had been well received and well cared for.

I sought the help of a friend who had become quite skilled at Internet research. Thanks to a relationship with a wayward boyfriend who "needed looking into," she had learned the shortest routes to public records such as marriage licenses, employment records, and property ownership.

"I don't want you to invade anyone's privacy or contact anyone," I assured her. "If you can just find me a current address for Jacqueline Eichelberger, I can go from there."

I gave her so little to go on, I thought a successful search would be unlikely. I provided a maiden name, an ex-husband's name, an address from 1980 and one from 1991.

The piece of paper my friend handed me when we met for lunch a few weeks later showed a long list of chronological life events that spanned twenty-three years. The trail ended at an address Jami's mother now shared with Jeff Eichelberger in South Charleston, Ohio, twelve miles from Jami's birthplace.

When I felt I had done as much research as I had a right to without Jami's mother's knowledge, it was time to either stop thinking about it and be content with what I had learned, or to contact Jacqueline.

I considered for several days whether I should write or call. If I sent a letter and received no acknowledgment, I would still have doubts. A voice on the phone would end my uncertainty. With a name and address in hand, a phone number would be easy enough to find.

I consulted AOL's white pages phone directory and found a number for J. Eichelberger at the address my friend had given me. I wrote it on a pink Post-It note and pressed it onto the handset of my desk phone. I glanced at it every time I wandered past, coming a little closer each time to picking up the receiver and dialing.

After a few days, on a Saturday afternoon, I sat down at my desk, determined not to walk away until I had made the call. I sat for more than an hour, staring at the telephone, rehearsing what I would say, imagining how Jami's mother might respond. Maybe she would be unable to deal with revisiting Jami's death. Maybe she would be angry that I hadn't thanked her twelve years earlier through the proper channels.

I considered the possibilities as I held the phone to my ear. I dialed and hoped for a busy signal, a no-longer-in-service squeal, or an unanswered ring. After four rings, I heard a woman's voice.

"Hello?"

Afraid I would lose courage, I abandoned my memorized lines and spoke quickly. "I'm not sure I've reached the right number. Is this Jacqueline Eichelberger?"

Her voice was hesitant, as though she thought she might be in for a telephone sales pitch. "Ye-es?"

"You don't know me, but I'm Carol Wilson, and I think you're the person who donated your daughter's kidney and pancreas to me twelve years ago."

She was silent for several seconds.

I added, "January 13, 1991. Have I reached the right person?"

The line was so quiet, I was sure I had made a terrible mistake—an error in judgment or a wrong turn in my research. She was going to hang up, I just knew it.

She finally spoke. "I'm sorry. I'm just so shocked to hear from you. Four other people were given Jami's organs, and I haven't heard from anyone else." She paused and then added, "Oh, I guess I wouldn't. We asked not to be contacted."

"Four others. That's wonderful," I said, pleased that she had been given at least some information about the recipients. Maybe that had been enough for her all this time. Maybe the lack of specifics had allowed her to move on.

I gave her the opportunity to end our conversation. "Well, I just wanted to call and thank you. It's long overdue. I hope I haven't upset you."

"I'm still in shock," she said quietly.

Now I could hear tears in her voice, and I knew she needed time to absorb what had just happened. I had given myself so much time to think about this first encounter. I had given her none. I wondered how she would deal with my call after it was over. I had needed to make it, but had failed to consider whether she had needed to receive it.

I gave Jacquie my e-mail address and encouraged her to write to me if she wanted to keep in touch. We said goodbye then and hung up, all of our questions unasked.

25

A week after my conversation with Jami's mother, I opened my e-mail and found a message titled *hello...Jacquie here (Jami's Mom)*. In the days following our talk, I thought I had accepted that I might not hear from Jacquie. But when I saw her e-mail, I realized how desperately I wanted to know more, not just about Jami, but about how her family had coped with her death. I needed to know they had survived intact, had found a way to move on. And it was more than that. I needed for them to know about me, that I was happy and well, that I was experiencing a life I had thought impossible, that their gift had been worthwhile.

I opened the mail and sat back in my chair while my computer read aloud to me.

Sep 16, 2003

Hi Carol,
Sorry I have not gotten back with you before now. It was really nice to hear from you. A shock, but nice. So.... how are you doing with your health? Everything okay? I have a lot of questions, and I'm sure you do too. Your family? Married? Children? Job?

I have to go for now. I have a home business and I'm busy this morning. Just wanted to make the time to drop you a line.
Have a great day!
Jacquie

I replied that afternoon, cautioning myself not to expect too much. Jami's family had been living a life for twelve years that had nothing to do with me. That life wouldn't stop in its tracks just because I had stepped in uninvited. I would have to be patient and let Jacquie decide where we would go from here. She had requested anonymity. If she asked again for privacy, I would honor her request.

My first note was short. I thanked Jacquie for her willingness to communicate with me, I confessed that I had searched public records for information about Jami, and I expressed sympathy for her loss. I would write more later, I told her, after a doctor appointment and dinner out with friends.

I wrote again the following morning, answering Jacquie's questions first. Married, no children, all of my family still in Ohio. I told her I was legally blind, so I didn't have a job away from home.

"But my health is good," I explained. "I've been free from insulin and diet since the day of my transplant. I still have some complications from my twenty-seven years with diabetes, but none related to my transplant. I'm able to do everything I need to do except drive a car and read fine print. I can read my computer screen and limited amounts of printed material with a handheld magnifier, and I get where I need to go locally by golf cart."

Enough about me, I decided. I closed by asking, "When you have time, please tell me about yourself. Your home business? Your family? Did Jami have siblings? Tell me anything you're comfortable talking about. Thanks for being in touch."

Jacquie wrote again early the next morning.

Sep 18, 2003

Good morning,
Well, where do I start?

Jami was born April 14, 1980. I always said she was my easy child. I had a doctor appointment at 3:00...she was born at 3:15! She was a good baby and kid. Smiled all the time. Loved to play sports...softball, basketball, and soccer...cheerleading when nothing else was going on.

I have been married three times. Jami has an older sister Kari, 31, and a younger sister Shari, 14.

Jami's father and I divorced when she was 5. When she was 7, I married my husband now...Jeff. Shari is mine and Jeff's. She was 2 when Jami died, and Kari was 18.

Jeff was one of Jami's basketball coaches. They were on their way to the first game of the season, January 5, 1991. Jeff slipped on ice and hit a van head on. I got the dreaded call from the hospital. Jeff had shattered his foot, and his eyelids were full of glass. Other than that, he was okay. Jami, on the other hand, had head and brain stem injuries. She was on life support and never did regain consciousness. On January 11, they told me she would always be that way. I could put her in a nursing home or shut the machines off. At 2:00 in the morning, January 12, God and I were "having it out," so to speak. I told Him, "You might be taking this one, but You are not going to take another one." At 2:30, I signed the papers to donate her organs, in hopes of saving another child who was dying somewhere.

Jami died at 1:15 P.M. on January 12. An 11 year old girl got her heart, a 36 year old woman, her liver, a 76 year old man, a kidney...and you. Someone got her eyes or part of them, not sure which.

We are all doing fine now. I have accepted it from day one. I had two choices...lay down and die also, or pick myself up, dust myself off, put one foot in front of the other...and move on. I had two girls at home, one a baby and one a teenager, and a husband who has to deal with this for the rest of his life...he was driving the car. Do I blame him? No, I don't. It was an accident. He is fine, but some years in early January, he gets really quiet. Some years I get kind of sad and quiet too. But then I just remember, it is also 5 other people's "birthday."

I collect angels now. Someone made a stained glass angel for Jami's funeral instead of sending flowers. That started it. I also wear angel pins...one every day.

But the best angel of my collection is my granddaughter. Her name is Angel Mari Jones. I didn't know that was going to be her name until the day she was born. Jami's middle name was Mari. Kari told me, "Mom, now you have your own live angel." She is seven now...and by no means an angel!"

Well, I'll stop here and get some things done. My business is business forms distribution. I have forms printed for 12 companies...checks, invoices, statements, etc. I've been in business for the past three years. Love it!

So I will talk to you later. Take care.

Jacquie

I was touched by Jacquie's openness and relieved by how at peace she sounded. Finally able to believe that my new beginning had not risen from the ashes of ruined lives, I held a new picture of a family getting through the day-to-day without anger or blame, an image of a mother celebrating the birthdays Jami had given to others, celebrating the birth of a grandchild named for Jami, and celebrating Jami's life every day with the wearing of an angel pin.

Jacquie and I wrote often for the next several months. Some of our notes were just brief hello's or holiday greetings. Others shared ordinary family news.

But the e-mails I looked forward to most were those in which Jacquie gave me glimpses of Jami's life. I looked for the Jami paragraphs and read them over and over, trying to know her better.

The moment Jami was born, she was sucking her thumb, not crying, eyes open and looking at me, so content. Her eyes were brown and her hair blonde. Her hair turned brown when she was about 7.

We lived in a half-double when Jami was born. Not a very good neighborhood, but not the worst either. When Jami was about six months old, we moved into one of Doug's dad's apartment houses, so Doug wouldn't have to pay any rent. This place was terrible. I complained long enough that we finally moved into a cute house. We only lived there a couple of months because Doug came home one day and told me he had joined the Army and we were moving to Monterey, California. And we did. Jami was about two. Jami, Kari, and I moved back to Ohio in 1985. Doug stayed behind, and we divorced in 1987.

I never talked bad about Jami's father in front of her. Jeff and I were always making excuses for him. After all, he is still her father. But he always put himself before his daughter, stepdaughter, and me. Jami got a Christmas present from Doug on the day of the accident, January 5. He was stationed in Georgia at the time. She never knew it came. That child looked for it in the mail every day for a week before Christmas and for the ten days that followed. I was going to go out and buy her something that Saturday to put in the mail for her from her dad, like I had before for birthdays and other Christmases.

Jami always told on herself when she did something she wasn't supposed to. One day when she was around four, she was in her room being way too quiet for a four-year-old. I yelled from the living room, "Jami, what are you doing in there?" She came out with her hands behind her back, stood in front of me and said, "Mommy, I didn't cut Ivory's whiskers off." Behind her back she was carrying a big pair of black-handled scissors. I ran into her bedroom and on her bed were eight whiskers all laid out in a row, and one mad cat!

I have always said God made Jami my "easy" child because He knew I wouldn't have her long. She was a real good kid. As a baby, she never cried, and I mean never. She laughed and smiled all the time. So many people came up to me at her funeral and talked about her beautiful smile, people I did not even know.

Jami loved softball (second base). On the third weekend of July, we have the Jami Snyder Memorial Fastpitch Softball Tournament. Started the year after Jami died, this will be our thirteenth year. The money goes toward scholarships for girls at the high school Jami would have graduated from...Northeastern.

I thought about Jami often that first winter after contacting Jacquie. On January 5, the day of her accident, I imagined her stepfather's grief, his memory of that icy disaster now thirteen years old. On January 11, I thought about Jacquie's decision to unplug the machines and sign the donor agreement that would save four lives. On January 12, when I saw an e-mail from Jacquie on my list, I left it there unopened until I had accomplished everything I needed to do for the day. I could only imagine what these anniversaries were like for Jacquie, what her letter would hold.

Jan 12, 2004

Hi Carol,
Well, today Jami has been gone for 13 years. Sometimes it seems that long and sometimes it seems like yesterday. Today is a good day for me. It's nice for the first time in 13 years to tell someone, "Happy (new) Birthday." It makes me feel better, puts a smile on my face.
Take care,
Jacquie

165

Jan 12, 2004

Dear Jacquie,
It was a beautiful day in Georgia today, nice enough finally for me to be out and about on my golf cart.
You have been in my thoughts all week. Mick and I will celebrate my "birthday" tomorrow. My family always remembers it too. Of course it will be a little different this year, now that I know more about you and Jami.
I remember when I was first placed on the transplant waiting list, a doctor told me to be especially prepared that winter, as so many transplant donations occur because of icy roads. It gave me kind of a sick feeling, as if I should prepare to benefit from someone else's loss. Maybe that's why for so long I needed to not consider where my kidney and pancreas came from. I just couldn't think about it. As it turns out, Jami did die in a winter car accident, as I always had a feeling she did.
Your note today has made it easier for me to feel at peace with the new life I received thirteen years ago and even with the way I received it. I hope you find peace today too, knowing that at least one of Jami's recipients is doing well. I don't know if you'll ever hear from others, but I know they must be grateful too.
I am blessed every day by your gift and by knowing you. Thank you!
Have a wonderful new year.
Carol

LaVergne, TN USA
23 June 2010
187199LV00001B/2/P